Abdoul Aziz Belemvire

Study of the impact of DDoS attacks on 4G/LTE mobile networks:

Abdoul Aziz Belemvire

Study of the impact of DDoS attacks on 4G/LTE mobile networks:

Analysis and innovative solutions for enhanced cybersecurity

Imprint

Any brand names and product names mentioned in this book are subject to trademark, brand or patent protection and are trademarks or registered trademarks of their respective holders. The use of brand names, product names, common names, trade names, product descriptions etc. even without a particular marking in this work is in no way to be construed to mean that such names may be regarded as unrestricted in respect of trademark and brand protection legislation and could thus be used by anyone.

Cover image: www.ingimage.com

This book is a translation from the original published under ISBN 978-3-639-52669-1.

Publisher:
Sciencia Scripts
is a trademark of
Dodo Books Indian Ocean Ltd. and OmniScriptum S.R.L publishing group

120 High Road, East Finchley, London, N2 9ED, United Kingdom
Str. Armeneasca 28/1, office 1, Chisinau MD-2012, Republic of Moldova, Europe
Managing Directors: Ieva Konstantinova, Victoria Ursu
info@omniscriptum.com

Printed at: see last page
ISBN: 978-620-8-37718-2

Dedication

I dedicate this work to all those who have supported me throughout this adventure. To Fadila SEMDE, for her invaluable help and sound advice throughout this project. Your encouragement and support enabled me to take decisive steps forward. To my family, for their unconditional love, unfailing support and confidence in me. You have been a constant source of motivation and inspiration.

Thanks

Throughout the pages of this memoir, I wish to express my deep gratitude to those who have been my guides, supporters and sources of inspiration throughout this exhilarating academic journey. To my teachers, whose patience and passion have illuminated my path, I offer my sincerest thanks. To my classmates, companions in challenges and discoveries, you have enriched my experience with your friendship and invaluable collaboration. Dr Désiré GUEL, we have accomplished everything together, and your dedication and expertise have been invaluable. To you, Dr Kiswendsida Kisito KABORÉ and Didier BASSOLE, I am grateful for your invaluable guidance and enlightened counsel. Finally, to myself, for meeting the challenges with determination and perseverance, I congratulate myself and celebrate this milestone in my academic career. May this memoir bear witness to our shared commitment to excellence and innovation. Thank you all for this unforgettable adventure.

Summary

4G/LTE mobile networks play a central role in modern communications infrastructures, offering fast, reliable connectivity. However, they are facing increasing threats, particularly distributed denial of service (DDoS) attacks, which compromise their availability and security. This study is part of a drive to better understand the impact of DDoS attacks on these networks, and to develop robust defense solutions. The aim is to identify the specific vulnerabilities of 4G/LTE networks to such attacks, and to propose appropriate countermeasures. The main objectives are to analyze attack mechanisms, assess their impact on quality of service, propose detection and mitigation techniques, and finally, strengthen network resilience in the face of future threats. The results obtained show that traditional and machine learning techniques can be effective, but require improvement to cope with new forms of attack. The case study presented uses the CIC-DDoS2019 dataset to evaluate these methods in 4G/LTE networks. The results highlight the importance of developing detection techniques adapted to these networks, while underlining the limitations of the dataset and the need to improve the quality of available data.

Keywords: dataset CIC-DDoS2019, attack detection, DDoS, 4G/LTE.

Table of contents

General introduction

The ubiquity of 4G/LTE mobile networks [1][1] has transformed the way we interact with the digital world, offering fast, reliable connectivity. However, this ubiquity has also paved the way for *cyber threats*[2] , among which *Distributed Denial of Service (DDoS)* attacks stand out as major challenges. This study aims to explore in depth the impact of these attacks on 4G/LTE mobile networks, identify inherent vulnerabilities, and propose robust security strategies to preserve the stability of these critical infrastructures.

Background and rationale

4G/LTE mobile networks are essential to the communications infrastructure, offering fast, reliable connectivity. However, with the rapid growth of Internet-based services, Distributed Denial of Service (DDoS) attacks represent a serious threat [2-4]. Understanding the specific impact of these attacks on 4G/LTE mobile networks is crucial to maintaining the quality of service and security of mobile communications.

The mass deployment of 4G/LTE mobile networks has radically changed the way individuals and businesses interact with communication services [1]. Although 4G/LTE offers high-speed connectivity and low latency, this has also attracted the attention of malicious actors, jeopardizing the availability and reliability of mobile networks.

DDoS attacks, with their ability to coordinate large-scale attacks from multiple sources, can cause significant service interruptions on 4G/LTE mobile networks, threatening quality of service. It is therefore imperative to understand in detail how these attacks affect these networks in order to develop robust defense mechanisms.

Motivations

The motivation for this study lies in the pressing need to better understand the consequences of *DDoS* attacks on 4G/LTE mobile networks. Understanding these impacts is of paramount importance, as it will enable the development of more effective defense mechanisms and the

---

1 *4G (Fourth Generation)/ LTE (Long-Term Evolution)* is the term commonly used in telecommunications to designate the latest standard in mobile network technology. The 4G/LTE network offers faster data speeds, lower latency and better overall performance than previous generations of mobile networks such as 3G.
2 *Cyber threats* are dangers, attacks or malicious actions targeting computer systems, networks, data and digital infrastructures. These threats can come from a variety of actors, such as hackers, criminal organizations, nation-states or ill-intentioned individuals.

implementation of appropriate security policies to protect these critical infrastructures. This research into the impact of DDoS attacks on 4G/LTE mobile networks is motivated by several crucial considerations.

(1) 4G/LTE mobile networks, despite their sophistication, are facing an increase in sophisticated DDoS attacks. It is crucial to understand these current and emerging vulnerabilities in order to develop effective security mechanisms to avoid service interruptions.

(2) The threat of Distributed Denial of Service (DDoS) attacks is not limited to just to disrupt online services, but can also serve as a diversion for more serious intrusions, compromising data security and user confidentiality. Awareness of the consequences of such attacks is essential to reinforce security measures aimed at protecting sensitive data.

(3) To develop effective countermeasures against DDoS attacks on mobile networks 4G/LTE, it's crucial to fully understand their impact. This deeper understanding will pave the way for the development of more effective strategies, such as early detection methods, strengthening network resilience, and rapid recovery protocols after an attack.

(4) The advent of 5G in mobile networks raises the need to learn from attacks DDoS on 4G/LTE networks to enhance the security of future infrastructures. This study is intended to guide the development of appropriate policies and solutions in the face of an ever-changing communications technology landscape.

Issues

The problem lies in identifying the specific vulnerabilities of 4G/LTE networks to these attacks, and proposing appropriate countermeasures. In this study, we will address the following questions concerning 4G/LTE mobile networks:

— What are the most common *DDoS* attack mechanisms used against 4G/LTE mobile networks?

— How do these attacks affect the availability and performance of mobile networks?

— What are the specific vulnerabilities of 4G/LTE networks to DDoS attacks?

— How to design effective countermeasures to mitigate the effects of DDoS attacks on 4G/LTE mobile networks

Objectives

As part of our study, we set ourselves several key objectives to better understand and address the challenges posed by DDoS attacks on 4G/LTE mobile networks.

1. First, we will analyze the types of DDoS attacks commonly directed against 4G/LTE mobile networks. This in-depth analysis of the different forms of attack will give us a better grasp of the underlying mechanisms and the predominant methods used by attackers.

2. We will then assess the impact of these attacks on the quality of service (QoS) of 4G/LTE networks. Our comprehensive assessment will enable us to quantify the disruption suffered by end-users, and identify the areas where network performance is most affected.

3. At the same time, we will identify specific vulnerabilities in 4G/LTE protocols exploited by DDoS attacks. By examining these protocols in detail, we will be able to identify potential flaws in communication protocols and propose effective security measures.

4. Finally, based on the results of our analyses, we will formulate practical recommendations for strengthening the resilience of 4G/LTE mobile networks against DDoS attacks. These strategies will include prevention, detection and mitigation measures, aimed at ensuring the availability and reliability of mobile communication services in a persistent threat environment.

Expected results

The expected results of this study go beyond simply identifying the impact of DDoS attacks. They move towards an in-depth understanding of DDoS attacks specifically targeted at 4G/LTE networks. This in-depth analysis will encompass attack methods, exploitation vectors and malicious traffic patterns specific to these complex environments. This understanding will form the fundamental basis for the development of appropriate countermeasures.

Consequently, the outcome of our project will include the proposal of innovative solutions aimed at strengthening the resilience of LTE mobile networks against DDoS attacks. These solutions will build on the lessons learned from the in-depth analysis, integrating DDoS attack detection mechanisms. The ultimate aim is to provide concrete, effective recommendations for optimizing the security of 4G/LTE networks in the face of the persistent threat of DDoS attacks.

Chapter 1: State of the art on DoS/DDoS attacks in 4G/LTE networks.

In this chapter, we present a state of the art on distributed denial of service (DoS/DDoS) attacks in 4G/LTE mobile networks. This exploration aims to provide a clear understanding of the fundamental concepts of DoS/DDoS attacks, as well as a review of the existing literature on the subject. This theoretical framework will serve as the basis for in-depth analyses and proposed solutions to enhance the security of mobile networks in the face of these threats.

1.1. Theoretical foundations of DoS/DDoS attacks

DoS/DDoS attacks represent a major threat to the availability and security of mobile networks. In this section, we define the key concepts related to DoS/DDoS attacks, focusing on their characteristics and operating mechanisms. A good understanding of these concepts is essential to grasp the scale of the risks and vulnerabilities inherent in 4G/LTE networks.

1.1.1 Definitions and key concepts

Denial of service (DoS) attacks and their *distributed* variant *(DDoS)* represent major threats to cybersecurity. In this section, we explore the differences between these two types of attack, as well as the key characteristics that define the formidable nature of DDoS attacks.

- *Definition and difference between DoS and DDoS attacks:* DDoS (distributed denial of service) attacks differ from classic DoS attacks in their ability to coordinate a concerted assault using a massive flow of malicious traffic from multiple sources, such as "zombies" or "botnets". This coordination makes the mitigation of DDoS attacks more complex than that of classic DoS attacks.

- *Characteristics:* DDoS attacks are defined by several key characteristics that make them formidable threats, including their scale, diversity, ability to morph and multiple objectives.

    - *Scale of attack:* DDoS attacks mobilize a large number of infected machines to generate a massive flow of traffic, often exceeding the capacity of the targeted system to handle it, resulting in slowdowns or total unavailability of services.

    - *Diversity of methods:* attackers use a variety of methods, targeting bandwidth or processing resources, making detection and mitigation complex.

    - *Metamorphosis and adaptability:* attackers constantly adjust their methods to evade detection by modifying traffic composition or changing source IP addresses.

    - *Multiple objectives:* DDoS attacks can have a variety of objectives, from simple disruption of services to more complex motivations, requiring in-depth understanding to develop effective countermeasures.

1.1.2   Mechanisms and techniques of DoS/DDoS attacks

DoS (Denial of Service) and DDoS (Distributed Denial of Service) attacks are designed to overwhelm an online service, network or computer system with illegitimate traffic, rendering the service inaccessible to legitimate users. Several mechanisms and techniques are used to execute these attacks:

(1)   Flood attack :
- Description: flood the target with a massive volume of network traffic.
- Example of a method: flooding UDP or ICMP packets.

(2)   TCP/IP exhaustion attack :
- Description: force the establishment of numerous TCP connections to saturate server resources.
- Example method: generate a large number of TCP connections to the target server.

(3)   Application Layer Attack :
- Description: exploit application vulnerabilities to drain server resources.
- Example of a method: send a large number of forged requests to a specific application.

(4)   Reflection Attack :
- Description: use third-party servers to amplify the attack.
- Example of a method: send fake requests to badly configured servers, which then send the answers back to the target.

(5)   Amplification Attack :
- Description: exploit misconfigured services to increase the power of the attack.
- Example of a method: using misconfigured memcached servers to amplify traffic.

(6)   DNS Flood attack :
- Description: overwhelm DNS servers with a large number of queries.
- Example of a method: send a large number of falsified DNS requests to the target DNS servers.

(7)   SSL/TLS Exhaustion attack :
- Description: saturate resources linked to SSL/TLS security protocols.
- Example of a method: send a large number of secure connection requests to target servers.

(8)   HTTP Exhaustion attack :
- Description: exhaust the HTTP resources of web servers with a large number of

requests.

- Example of a method: send a large number of HTTP requests to target web servers.

In summary, this exploration of the different typologies of DDoS attacks provides an insight into the diversity and complexity of the methods employed by attackers to disrupt online services. A thorough understanding of these strategies is an essential foundation on which to build robust, proactive defense strategies, a topic we will address in the next section.

1.2 Literature review

1.2.1 Security architecture for 4G/LTE networks against DoS/DDoS attacks

In this section, we present an overview of the 4G/LTE network architecture and its security mechanism. This section provides a basic understanding of DoS/DDoS attacks on 4G/LTE networks.

1.2.1.1 Security architecture for 4G/LTE networks

Security in 4G/LTE networks is a crucial aspect in guaranteeing the integrity, confidentiality and availability of the services offered. This section provides a detailed overview of the security architecture of these networks, highlighting the different layers of protection and key management mechanisms used to counter potential threats.

1.2.1.2 General architecture of 4G/LTE networks

The 4G/LTE network [5] is based on the architecture shown in figure I.1.

It consists of a radio access network called *E-UTRAN*[3] and a network core. *The E- UTRAN is made up of several advanced nodes (e-NodeBs)*, which have the function of B nodes and assume most of the Radio Network Controller functions in the UTRAN. *The User Equipment (UE)* and the e-NodeB are connected via the radio interface *(Uu interface)*[4] . The e-NodeBs are

---

3 *E-UTRAN (Evolved Universal Terrestrial Radio Access Network)* is a fundamental component of the 4G/LTE network. It is the radio access network that evolved from 3GPP's UMTS *(Universal Mobile Telecommunication System)*.

4 The radio interface *(Uu interface)* is the wireless link between the UE and the eNodeB in the LTE network.

connected to each other via *the X2 interface*[5][6] and mainly implement the following functions: radio resource management, IP header compression and user data encryption, connection to *the Mobility Management Entity (MME)* via the *S1-MME4* interface, and connection to the *Service Gateway (SGW)* via *the S1-U interface*[7] . In addition, 4G/LTE takes

---

5 *The X2 interface* is a communication interface dedicated to the exchange of data between two base stations (eNodeBs). This interface enables neighboring base stations to coordinate their activities and ensure a smooth transition of users between cells.

6 *S1-MME* is an interface used to connect the eNodeB to the Mobility Management Entity (MME) in LTE networks. It enables mobility management, user standby and transfer of *Non Access Stratum (NAS)* signaling, etc.

7 S1-U is the interface used in LTE networks to connect the eNodeB to the *Serving Gateway (SGW)*. It carries user data traffic between the eNodeB and the core network. The S1-U interface is responsible for

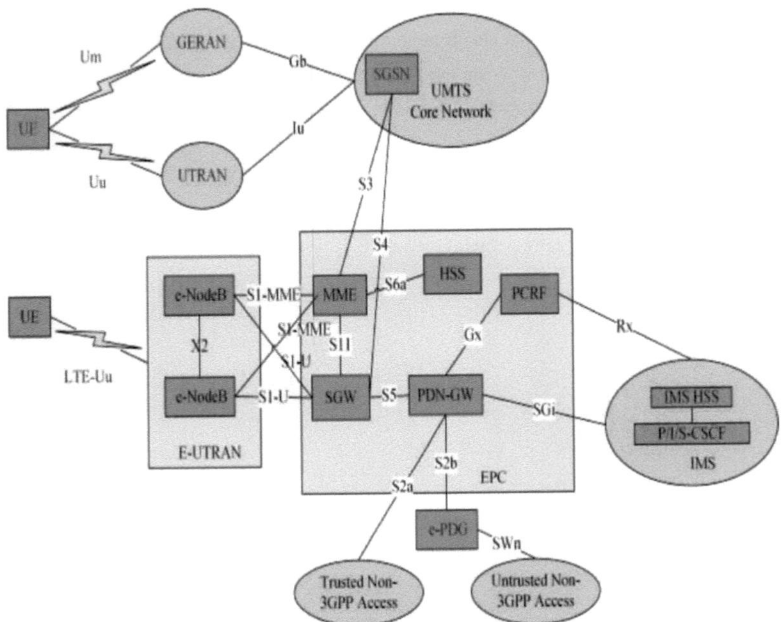

FIGURE I.1 - General architecture of 4G/LTE networks [1].

also *supports HeNBs (Home eNodeBs)*[8 9 10] and *Relay Nodes (RN)*[11] , and when a large number of HeNBs are deployed, a Home Base Station Gateway must be deployed. The core of the 4G/LTE network is called the EPC network. It provides connections to several heterogeneous access networks, including 3GPP access networks *(E-UTRAN, GERAN and UTRAN)*[12] and non-3GPP access networks *(WiMAX*[13] *, CDMA2000, etc.).* The Evolved Packet Core (EPC) is the central network architecture of 4G/LTE networks, and comprises the Mobility Management Entity (MME), which is responsible for managing signaling and user mobility aspects, the Home Subscriber Server (HSS), the SGW, the Packet Data Gateway (PDN-GW) and the Policy and Pricing Rules Function (PCRF).

The EPC separates the control surface from the user surface. The MME performs the functions of the control surface and the SGW performs the functions of the user surface. The MME hosts the following functions: NAS signaling, NAS signaling security, Access Stratum (AS) security control, standby mobility management, bearer control, etc., while the HSS provides services for the 4G/LTE core network and the IMS network as a central database. The MME connects to the HSS via the S6a interface to transfer authentication data. The main functions of the SGW are routing and forwarding. The PDN-GW is primarily for UE IP address allocation, packet filtering and legitimate monitoring. The PCRF is mainly for flow-based charging and network control of service data flow detection to guarantee Quality of Service (QoS). Non 3GPP Trusted and Untrusted Access Networks are IP access networks whose specifications are outside the 3GPP domain. The functionality of the Evolved Packet Data Gateway (e-PDG) includes allocation and transport of a remote IP address, a local mobility anchor in untrusted access networks, authentication and tunnel authorization, and so on.

In the 4G/LTE network, the IMS network is used to manage packet-switched services such as VoLTE. In addition, GSM and UMTS networks support circuit-switched fallback procedures

---

the transfer of user data packets to and from the SGW, thus ensuring that the data are transmitted efficiently and reliably.

10 *HeNBs or Home eNodeBs* are also known as femtocells.
11 *Relay Nodes (RN)* refer to network elements that act as data relays between base stations (eNodeBs) and the core network. These relay nodes are also known as *eNodeB relays (eNB-R)* or *Relay Nodes (RN)*.
12 *E-UTRAN, GERAN and UTRAN* are key components of 4G/LTE networks. *E-UTRAN (Evolved Universal Terrestrial Radio Access Network)* is the radio access network for LTE technology, GERAN *(GSM EDGE Radio Access Network)* is used for GSM and EDGE technologies, while *UTRAN (Universal Terrestrial Radio Access Network)* was the radio access network used in UMTS systems. These networks play a crucial role in the provision of mobile communication services across different generations of wireless technologies.
13 WiMAX (Worldwide Interoperability for Microwave Access) is a broadband wireless communications technology designed to provide high-speed Internet access over long distances. It operates on radio frequencies between 2 GHz and 11 GHz, enabling extensive coverage and high-speed data transmission.

(CSFB). This can be triggered when the IMS is not in use. IMS is a powerful framework deployed by the LTE/LTE-A network to provide different types of multimedia services such as VoLTE, Short Messaging Service (SMS), streaming video, etc. The IMS is made up of user, control and application planes. The user plane is a Session Initiation Protocol (SIP) application inserted in the devices. The main function of the control plane is session control. The control plane comprises the Call Session Control Function (CSCF) and the HSS. The CSCF can be divided into Proxy Call Session Control Functions (P-CSCF), Interrogation Call Session Control Functions (I-CSCF) and Service Call Session Control Functions (S-CSCF). Each has an IP address visible in the Domain Name Service (DNS). The P-CSCF is the first point connected when the user connects to the IMS network, forwarding SIP registration requests and SIP messages to the SIP server. The I-CSCF assigns an S-CSCF to each user performing a SIP registration, and routes incoming requests to the assigned S-CSCF. The S-CSCF performs session control services, such as SIP registration and incoming service requests. The HSS holds IMS user information and performs user authentication in the user registration process. The application plane is made up of application servers that can provide different services such as VoLTE, SMS, etc. The transmission of signaling data in the IMS is based on SIP, and packet data is mainly transmitted on the basis of the Real-Time Transport Protocol (RTP). The SIP layer is of great importance in IMS, controlling various multimedia services. But it presents several vulnerabilities due to its text-based nature, which means that the IMS system could suffer from SIP-related attacks.

1.2.1.3   4G/LTE network security

In this section, we begin with an overview of the security architecture of these networks, followed by the security key hierarchy and transfer key management in the context of 4G/LTE. Finally, we look at the security of the *IP Multimedia Subsystem* (IMS).

- *4G/LTE network security architecture:* This section describes the five security levels defined by 3GPP [6] to meet certain threats and security requirements. As shown in Figure 1.2, these levels include network access security *(I)*, network domain security *(II)*, user domain security *(III)*, application domain security *(IV), and* security visibility and configurability *(V)*.

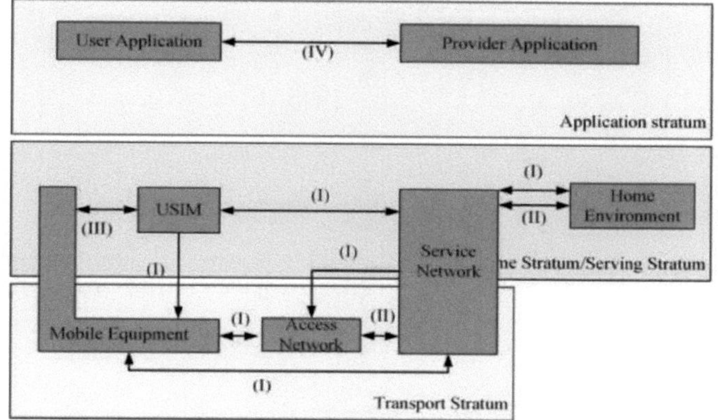

FIGURE I.2 - 4G/LTE network security architecture (Source [1])

— *Security key hierarchy:* 4G/LTE networks use a key derivation function to generate various keys, as illustrated in Figure I.2. These keys include K (permanent master key), CK and IK *(encryption and integrity keys), KASME (session key shared between UE and MME), KeNB (encryption key for node B), KNASint* and *KNASenc (keys to protect NAS traffic),* as well as *KUPenc* and *KRRCint/KRRCenc (keys to protect radio resource control and user traffic).*

— *Transfer key management:* This section deals with transfer key management for inter-radio access technology transfers and intra-E-UTRAN transfers. It details the procedures for intra- and inter-MME transfers, with particular emphasis on key separation to guarantee security during transfers.

— *IMS security:* Before users can access multimedia services, *EPS-AKA[14]* and *IMS-AKA[15]* must be authenticated. The IMS assigns a new

---

[14] *EPS-AKA (Evolved Packet System-Authentication and Key Agreement)* is a protocol used in 4G/LTE networks for authentication and security key establishment between the user device (and the core network *(EPC, Evolved Packet Core).* The EPS-AKA process is an evolution of the AKA (Authentication and Key Agreement) protocol used in earlier mobile networks, such as 3G.

[15] *IMS-AKA (IP Multimedia Subsystem Authentication and Key Agreement)* is a mechanism used in 4G/LTE networks to authenticate and exchange security keys between the user and the telecommunications network. It is part of the authentication and security management protocol defined by 3GPP for 4G/LTE networks.

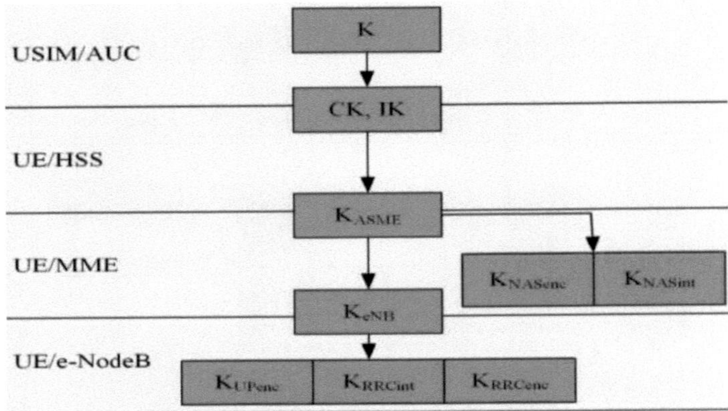

FIGURE I.3 - 4G/LTE security key hierarchy (Source [1])

subscriber identity module (ISIM) at each UE, storing the IMS authentication keys required for secure exchanges.

1.2.1.4 Security key hierarchy in 4G/LTE networks

The 4G/LTE network [1] uses the key derivation function to derive various keys. The hierarchy is shown in Figure I.3 as follows:

— K is a permanent master key securely stored in both the USIM and the *Authentication Center (AuC)*[16] .

— *CK*[17] and *IK*[18] are encryption and integrity keys derived in *the USIM* and *AuC* from *K* for encryption and integrity verification, respectively.

— *KASME*[19] is derived from CK and IK, and is shared between the UE and the MME to

---

16 *The Authentication Center (AuC)*, also known as the Home Location Register (HLR/AuC), is an essential component of mobile telecommunications networks. The AuC is responsible for managing authentication and security information for a network operator's mobile subscribers.

17 *CK (Ciphering Key)* is the encryption key used to encrypt user data *(such as voice calls, text messages, Internet data)* prior to transmission over the radio interface between the user device and the LTE base station (eNodeB). Data encryption with CK guarantees the confidentiality of information exchanged over the wireless network.

18 *IK (Integrity Key)* is the integrity key used to generate *Integrity Check Value (ICV)* codes, which are transmitted with user data over the radio interface. ICVs are used to check the integrity of data when it is received by the LTE base station, thus ensuring that it has not been altered or modified during transmission.

19 *KASME* is the universal mobility authentication session key *(Key for Authentication and Security Management Entity)*. In LTE, the KASME key is derived from the *encryption key (CK)* and the *integrity key*

generate a series of session keys.

— *KeNB (Key eNodeB)* is derived in the EU and the MME or a target e-NodeB from *KASME* depending on the state of the EU.

— *KNASint*[20] and *KNASenc*[21] are a pair of keys derived by the UE and MME from KASME to protect NAS traffic.

— *KUPenc* is derived in the UE and e-NodeB from *KeNB* to protect user plane traffic. Securing these keys is essential to prevent DoS/DDoS attacks, as they protect the network's vital communication channels.

1.2.1.5 Handover key management in 4G/LTE networks

Key management during handover transitions between 4G/LTE cells comprises two types of intra-E-UTRAN handover: *intra-MME handover*[22] and *inter-MME handover*[23] . Intra-MME handover occurs between two e-NodeBs connected to the same MME via the X2 interface, while inter-MME handover involves the MME via the S1 interface. Inter-MME handover always uses the full *EPS-AKA* procedure to ensure a secure environment, whereas intra-MME handover simply transfers a new KeNB from a source e-NodeB to a target e-NodeB. To ensure security, back-end key separation is achieved using a one-way hash function, preventing the e-NodeB from deriving past session keys from current ones. In addition, forward key separation is required to prevent the source e-NodeB from predicting the target e-NodeB's key. This is achieved by using the Next Hop (NH) key and the *NH chaining counter (NCC)* to generate new keys. The KeNB key can be derived using two procedures:

horizontal or vertical derivation. The first procedure derives the KeNB key from the previous KeNB when there is no fresh *(NH, NCC)* pair or when the NCC value in the source eNodeB is not less than that received from the MME. The second, more common and secure procedure, uses the

---

(IK). These two keys are supplied by the operator's network and are used to secure communications between the UE and the LTE network.

20 KNASint is the *NAS* security key *(NAS Integrity)*. The KNASint key is used to guarantee the integrity of messages exchanged between the UE and the network at the NAS layer.

21 *KNASenc* is the *NAS* security key *(NAS Encryption)*. This key is used to encrypt messages exchanged between the UE and the network at the NAS layer in 4G/LTE networks.

22 *Intra-MME" (Mobility Management Entity) handover* is the process of continuously transferring a user's data session between different radio cells, while maintaining the connection with the same MME in the LTE network.

23 *Inter-MME (Mobility Management Entity) handover* is a crucial process in 4G/LTE networks, enabling the seamless transfer of a user's communication session from one MME to another, while maintaining connectivity and quality of service.

NH key received from the MME to derive the KeNB key when the NCC value in the source eNodeB is lower than that received from the MME.

1.2.1.6 IMS security

Key management during handover transitions between 4G/LTE cells is essential to ensure service continuity. Before a user can access multimedia services, *EPS-AKA* and *IMS-AKA* authentication must be performed [1, 7]. In the IMS context, each user benefits from a new *IMS* identification module *(ISIM)* similar to the *USIM* used to connect to the 4G/LTE network. The ISIM stores the IMS authentication keys and their associated functions. *The S-CSCF[24]* processes user authentication requests using the HSS, which holds a copy of the IMS authentication keys. However, this procedure presents potential security vulnerabilities, particularly during handovers. Appropriate security measures must be put in place to protect sensitive information exchanged during these transitions, such as data encryption and message integrity verification.

1.2.2 Taxonomy of DoS/DDoS attacks specific to 4G/LTE networks

In this section, we present a taxonomy of DoS/DDoS attacks specific to 4G/LTE networks, which has also been proposed by He et al [1]. Indeed, the 4G/LTE network deployed worldwide for its excellent performance is nevertheless facing new threats due to new features in its architecture [5, 6] such as *IP connectivity[25]* and *full interoperability with heterogeneous wireless access networks.* The 4G/LTE attacks proposed over the last decade are summarized in this section. Figure I.4 describes the taxonomy of 4G/LTE attacks as a function of network structure.

---

24 *S-CSCF (Serving-Call Session Control Function)* is a key element of the IP Multimedia Subsystem (IMS) architecture, used to provide multimedia services over LTE networks.

25 *IP connectivity* in 4G/LTE is based on a set of protocols and technologies that enable devices to connect to the LTE network, establish data sessions, route IP packets and guarantee quality of service (QoS) for different applications and traffic types.

Category	Subcategory	Attacks
Access Network	Disclosure of IMSI	
	Location Tracking	
	FR Jamming Spoofing & Sniffing De-Synchronization Attacks	
	DoS/DDoS Attacks	Botnet-Launched DDoS Attacks Signaling DoS Attacks
	Rogue Base Station Attacks	
	Other Attacks	Replay Attacks Eavesdropping Attacks
Core Network	DoS/DDoS Attacks Insider Attacks	Overload of HSS Overload of SGW
IMS Network	SIP-Related Attacks	Attacks in VoLTE SIP Flooding DoS Attacks Silent Call Attacks
		VoLTE Spamming, Spoofing & Phishing SMS Spamming, Spoofing SMS Powered Services Attacks
	Attacks in SMS Abnormal Charging in VoLTE TCP/SYN Flooding Attacks SQL Injection Attacks	
User Equipment	Mobile Botnet Mobile Malware	

Figure I.4 - Taxonomy of attacks on 4G/LTE networks [1].

1.2.2.1 Attacks on the access network

In this section we focus on significant attacks on the 4G/LTE access network, with a particular emphasis on DoS/DDoS attacks.

— *Disclosure of International Mobile Subscriber Identity (IMSI)*: IMSI is a permanent identifier of a subscriber, which must be transmitted as infrequently as possible to guarantee confidentiality of identity. 4G/LTE specifications minimize the frequency at which IMSI is transmitted over the radio interface. Disclosure of the IMSI can leak information about the subscriber, his location and even his conversations, enabling attackers to launch DoS attacks [8]. Several attacks to obtain the IMSI have been proposed in the literature, such as those described by Rao et al [9] and Holtmanns et al [10].

— *Location tracking*: cell phone users' location data is considered private personal information. Advances in positioning technologies and location-based services also pose a threat to user privacy. Location disclosure attacks have been described by Rao et al [9] and Holtmanns et al [10], exploiting protocols such as *Instantaneous Downlink Rate (IDR)*[26] and *User Data Rate (UDR)*[27] .

— *RF jamming, spoofing and interception*: wireless networks are vulnerable to RF jamming, spoofing and interception attacks, which can cause DoS attacks by lowering the signal-to-noise ratio of received signals. Attacks such as jamming synchronization signals and jamming physical control channels have been identified [11-13].

— *DoS/DDoS attacks*: DoS and DDoS attacks are serious for 4G/LTE networks, and can be launched by individual attackers or botnets[28] . Methods such as RF jamming attacks and control channel jamming attacks can cause DoS attacks. DDoS attacks can exploit limited network resources and affect services for legitimate users [2, 14].

— *Desynchronization attacks*: desynchronization attacks have been proposed, aimed at disrupting the management of intra-MME transfers. Han and Choi [15] described a desynchronization attack scheme aimed at compromising the key transfer process.

— *Fake base station attacks*: attacks using fake base stations can be used for location tracking, DoS attacks and even man-in-the-middle (MITM) attacks [16].

— *Other attacks*: in addition to those mentioned, other attacks such as replay attacks and eavesdropping attacks exist, representing potential threats to network security [17].

1.2.2.2   Attacks on the core network

In this section, we explore the different types of attack on the 4G/LTE core network.

— *DoS/DDoS attacks*: attacks on core network elements are a serious threat to normal data transmission in the 4G/LTE network. Mobile botnets can be used to launch DDoS attacks

---

26 *Instantaneous data rate (IDR)* refers to the actual data transmission rate on the wireless cana in a 4G/LTE network.

27 *User Data Rate (UDR)* is the average data transfer rate experienced by the user over a period of time in a 4G/LTE network.

28 Botnets" refer to networks of compromised devices (such as smartphones, tablets; or IoT devices) that have been infected with malware, often without their owners' knowledge. These; compromised devices, also known as "bots" or "zombies", can be remotely controlled by a central server, usually operated by cybercriminals.

on the access network, but also to flood core network elements such as the MME, SGW and PDN-GW by repeatedly initiating attachment procedures [2].

HSS overload: the HSS plays a crucial role in the EPC, storing subscriber information such as IMSIs, billing and account information, as well as authentication keys. Overloading the HSS could affect network service performance, for example by constantly sending false IMSIs to the HSS.

SGW overload: several cases of SGW overload are presented, including the massive sending of session configuration messages or the frequent triggering of TAU procedures.

— *Insider attacks*: insider attacks are often overlooked, but can be carried out by individuals with access privileges to specific network elements, disrupting normal communications in the 4G/LTE core network. For example, an insider could physically or remotely shut down a network node in the core network, or turn off a base station [14].

1.2.2.3   Attacks on IMS

The IMS system suffers from various SIP-related attacks because the SIP protocol is context-based, and the IMS system is vulnerable to many common Internet attacks because of its connectivity to the Internet. In this section we review some SIP-related attacks and their extension to IMS services.

— *SIP-related attacks in IMS :*
  (i)   The most serious attacks in the IMS are SIP-related, such as SIP flooding attacks. These attacks can be launched by sending a large quantity of SIP messages, such as SIP REGISTER[29] or SIP INVITE[30] messages with a falsified source IP address, in order to cause resource exhaustion and Denial of Service (DoS) attacks [18].
  (ii) SIP messages are easily decoded, enabling attackers to modify, distort or forge SIP messages to launch attacks such as forged SIP message injection [18].
— *Attacks on VoLTE:*
  (i)   *SIP DoS flooding attacks:* an attacker can send a large quantity of SIP messages to the P-CSCF using numerous devices to exhaust VoLTE service resources [19].
  (ii) *Silent call attacks:* an attacker can send call signalling messages to a victim, forcing it to remain in a high-power DRR state, which can quickly drain the victim's battery

---

29 "SIP REGISTER" is the message registering a mobile/terminal with the SIP *(Session Initiation Protocol)* server. SIP is a signaling protocol used to initiate, maintain and terminate real-time sessions such as voice and video calls over IP networks.

30 "SIP INVITE" is the SIP *(Session Initiation Protocol)* message sent to initiate a communication session, such as a voice call or multimedia session.

[20].

     (iii) VoLTE spamming: an attacker can use automatic calling systems to randomly call normal subscribers and transmit commercial messages [21].

     (iv) VoLTE spoofing: an attacker can modify the caller's number in the SIP message header to deceive the victim [21].

     (v) VoLTE phishing: the spoofing attacks mentioned above can be used to deceive the victim and cause financial harm [21].

— *Attacks on SMS :*

     (i) SMS spamming: SMS spam are unwanted messages sent to mobile devices [22, 23].

     (ii) SMS spoofing: an attacker can send messages on behalf of another cell phone user without their consent [22, 23].

     (iii) Attacks on SMS services: companies often use SMS to interact with their customers, but these services can be subject to attacks such as account hijacking[22, 23].

— *Abnormal billing in VoLTE:* attacks can exploit the lack of access control in VoLTE to obtain free access to VoLTE services or to carry out denial-of-service attacks [24, 25].

— *TCP/SYN flooding attacks:* these attacks exploit vulnerabilities in the TCP protocol to launch denial-of-service (DoS) attacks.

— *SQL injection attacks:* SQL injection attacks enable attackers to modify data in SIP proxies, causing a denial of service in the authentication procedure between the UE and the P-CSCF.

1.2.2.4 Attacks on user equipment (UE) or mobile devices

Mobile security is also of great importance in 4G/LTE security. The main security threats to mobiles are *mobile botnets* and *mobile malware.*

Mobile botnets are a powerful attack on mobile networks, launched by a large number of infected mobile devices. In addition to denial-of-service (DoS/DDoS) attacks, botnets can also steal data from bots to a *botnet master*[31] . The most common command channel in the 4G/LTE network is SMS, since SMS is widely used. There are many approaches to sending SMS cost-effectively, such as some web interfaces that provide free SMS services. In this way, the SMS-based mobile botnet becomes efficient and cost-effective [1].

---

31 In the context of 4G/LTE networks, the term *"botnet master"* refers to the controller or operator of a botnet, i.e. a network of compromised devices *(often called bots)* that are controlled and coordinated remotely to carry out malicious activities such as launching distributed denial-of-service (DDoS) attacks, spreading malware or stealing sensitive information.

Mobile malware has a serious impact on LTE/LTE- A network security, being able to be exploited by attackers to launch attacks such as denial-of-service (DoS) attacks, mobile botnet attacks, SMS spam attacks and abnormal billing attacks. In addition, mobile malware can execute malicious behaviors including backdoor creation, theft of sensitive data and elevation of privileges [1].

Conclusion

In this chapter we proposed an in-depth analysis of DoS/DDoS attacks on 4G/LTE networks, starting with an exploration of the theoretical underpinnings of these attacks. We then clarify the differences between DoS and DDoS attacks, highlighting the increased complexity of DDoS attacks due to their ability to coordinate large-scale attacks from multiple sources. The key characteristics of DDoS attacks are also examined, including their scale, diversity, ability to metamorphose and multiple objectives.

We then turn to the security architecture of 4G/LTE networks, providing a detailed overview of the network architecture and its security mechanisms. Examination of the security key hierarchy in 4G/LTE networks highlights the importance of key management during handover transitions between LTE cells, with a particular focus on IMS security. Finally, in this chapter we explore attacks on the access network, core network, IMS and mobile devices, highlighting significant threats such as mobile botnets and mobile malware.

Chapter 2: Techniques for detecting DDOS attacks on 4G/LTE networks

2.1. DDoS attack detection techniques

Before DDoS attacks in 4G/LTE networks can be effectively countered, robust detection methods and techniques are imperative. This section will therefore look at the different approaches used to detect these specific attacks, providing an essential overview of the defense strategies available in the context of mobile communications (Table II.1).

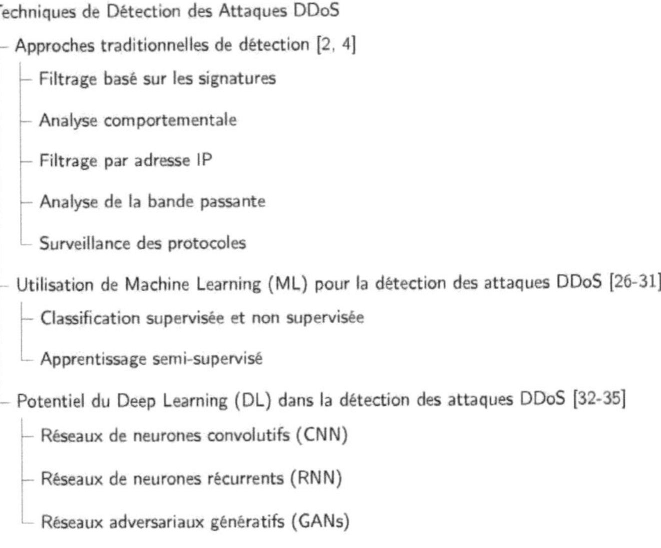

FIGURE II.1 - Classification of DDoS attack detection techniques

2.1.1 Traditional detection approaches

In this subsection, we look at the classic methods used before the advent of machine learning and deep learning techniques. These approaches generally rely on predefined rules and detection thresholds to identify DDoS attacks. These approaches generally focus on mechanisms for filtering abnormal or suspicious traffic, using techniques such as :

— *Signature-based filtering:* this approach relies on the comparison of observed traffic with pre-established signatures of malicious behavior. When a match is detected, the activity is identified as a DDoS attack [2].

— *Behavioral analysis:* this approach monitors the behavior of traffic on the network and identifies anomalies based on pre-established patterns. For example, a sudden increase in traffic to a single destination may indicate a DDoS attack [2].

— *Filtering by IP address:* this method involves blocking traffic from IP addresses that are suspect or identified as potential sources of DDoS attacks. This can be based on blacklists of IP addresses known to be associated with attacks [2].

— *Bandwidth analysis:* by monitoring and analyzing network bandwidth, DDoS attacks can be detected by identifying unusual peaks or abnormal traffic patterns [4].

— *Protocol monitoring:* this approach focuses on analyzing network protocols to detect anomalies or non-compliant behavior that could indicate a DDoS attack [4].

These traditional approaches to DDoS attack detection [2, 4], while effective in many cases, can be limited in terms of their ability to detect new forms of attack or to handle very high traffic loads.

2.1.2   Using machine learning to detect DDoS attacks

The use of machine learning techniques has shown promise in detecting and mitigating *distributed denial-of-service (DDoS)* attacks, which are a persistent threat to modern communication networks, including 4G/LTE networks. Several research studies [26-31] have explored this approach in the specific context of LTE networks.

Ayyaz et al [26] have proposed a novel security system to prevent DoS attacks on 4G LTE networks. Their approach implements machine learning mechanisms to monitor and detect malicious activity, offering protection against DDoS attacks.

Bahashwan et al. in [27] take an in-depth look at machine learning (ML) and deep learning (DL) approaches for detecting DDoS attacks in software-defined networks (SDNs). Although the study offers a comprehensive overview of existing work, it could benefit from a more critical analysis of the quality of the data used in the primary studies. In addition, the article highlights the need to resolve the remaining challenges, but a more detailed discussion of potential solutions would have been rewarding.

As for Setia et al. in [28], they propose a novel architectural framework for capturing and analyzing network flows in *VANET Cloud* environments[1] using machine learning techniques for classification and predictive analysis of DDoS attacks. The focus[32] is on improving the security of *VANET Cloud* deployments, with attack detection accuracy reaching 99.59%. However, despite these promising results.

The study by Sharif et al [29] addresses the detection of application-layer DDoS attacks, focusing on the use of various freely available DDoS attack tools. The study uses machine learning to detect these attacks, with a feature selection technique to improve model efficiency. The results show impressive performance, with an accuracy of 96%, a recall score of 98% and an F1 score of 97%.

Almaraz-Rivera et al. 2022 make a significant contribution in [30] to the detection of DDoS attacks on IoT networks using machine learning and deep learning models. The study highlights the growing importance of security in an increasingly connected IoT ecosystem highlighting the need to detect these attacks effectively and quickly. The authors propose an approach based on machine learning (ML) and deep learning (DL) to detect DDoS attacks at the transport and application layers.

Alashhab et al. in the study *"A Survey of Low Rate DDoS Detection Techniques Based on Machine Learning in Software-Defined Networks"* [31], explores techniques for detecting *low-rate DDoS (LDDoS)* attacks[33] in software-defined networks (SDNs) using machine learning approaches. The study highlights the growing importance of security in SDNs due to their widespread adoption and centralized architecture, while also highlighting the specific challenges posed by LDDoS attacks.

One of the strengths of this study [31] lies in its comprehensive approach to examining different LDDoS attack detection techniques using machine learning in SDN networks. By focusing on the use of machine learning, the authors reflect an innovative approach to the challenge posed by LDDoS attacks, which require more sophisticated detection techniques than traditional DDoS attacks. This approach highlights the growing importance of integrating artificial intelligence into network security to deal with increasingly complex threats.

Overall, these studies [26-31] highlight the potential effectiveness of machine learning for detecting DDoS attacks in 4G/LTE networks.

---

32 *VANET Cloud* refers to the integration of *Vehicle Ad-Hoc Networks (VANETs)* with a cloud computing infrastructure. VANETs are networks made up of vehicles equipped with communication devices, enabling them to communicate with each other and with road infrastructures.

33 *LDDoS (Low-and-Slow Denial of Service)* is a type of cyber attack designed to disrupt the availability of a targeted system or network. Unlike traditional Denial of Service (DoS) attacks, which flood the target with a high volume of traffic over a short period of time, LDDoS attacks are more subtle and aim to exhaust the target's resources over an extended period.

2.1.3 The potential of Deep Learning (DL) for detecting DDoS attacks

In this subsection, we analyze the potential of *Deep Learning (DL)*-based techniques in detecting DDoS attacks in 4G/LTE networks. *Deep Learning (DL)* techniques have the ability to identify anomalies in network traffic data in complex patterns. Deep neural networks can be trained to recognize malicious behavior without the need for attack-specific rules.

In the literature, Ahmadi et al [32] proposed a scheme for detecting and predicting DDoS attacks in a *Real Urban IoT Environment* using *Federated Deep* Learning[34] . Their model exploits the capabilities of Deep Learning to analyze traffic patterns and detect anomalies associated with DDoS attacks. They have demonstrated that their approach achieves high performance in terms of accuracy and loss rate (accuracy and loss rates of 0.953 and 0.0369 respectively), while preserving the confidentiality of traffic data.

Roopak et al [33] proposed Deep Learning models for cybersecurity in IoT networks, focusing in particular on DDoS attack detection. Their models were evaluated using real datasets *(CICIDS2017 [35])* and showed high accuracy in detecting DDoS attacks. The authors claim to have achieved a DDoS attack detection accuracy of 97.16% using the *CICIDS2017* datasets, while comparing their models with traditional machine learning algorithms, demonstrating the superior effectiveness of Deep Learning in this context.

Gupta et al [34] propose an interesting perspective based on Big Data and Deep Learning to detect DDoS attacks in a cloud computing environment. Their technique combines large-scale data analysis with Deep Learning algorithms to filter out malicious packets. They used the *KDDCUP99* dataset[35] to train and test their model, achieving a high accuracy of 99.73% in detecting DDoS attacks.

All the work [32-34] reported in this section highlights the ability of Deep Learning to detect DDoS attacks rather effectively in a variety of environments , ranging from smart city networks to IoT networks and cloud computing environments. Thanks to their ability to learn complex patterns and generalize from data, Deep Learning models offer a promising approach to strengthening network security against DDoS attacks in 4G/LTE networks.

---

34 *Federated Deep Learning (FDL)* is an emerging approach to machine learning and deep learning that addresses the privacy and scalability challenges associated with traditional centralized learning systems. In federated learning, instead of collecting and aggregating data on a central server, the learning process is decentralized and takes place locally on individual devices or nodes.

35 *KDD Cup 1999* is a well-known data set used in benchmarking and research in the field of intrusion detection and network security.

2.2.   Data collection and pre-processing

Having examined the various techniques for detecting DDoS attacks, we now turn to the section on data collection and pre-processing, which is a crucial step in the implementation of these techniques.

2.2.1   Data sources

As part of the detection of DDoS attacks in 4G/LTE networks, several data sources are used to gather relevant information on network traffic and equipment behavior. The main data sources include:

— Network traffic data

This data includes information on network traffic generated by both legitimate users and attackers. It can be collected from network gateways, switches, routers and other intermediate devices in the 4G/LTE network. Network traffic data provides details of communication patterns, data volumes exchanged and protocols used, making it possible to identify potential anomalies associated with DDoS attacks.

— Network equipment logs

Logs from network equipment, such as firewalls, proxy servers and intrusion detection systems (IDS), provide detailed records of events on the network. These logs may contain information on established connections, rejected requests, suspicious authentication attempts and so on. By analyzing these logs, we can detect early signs of DDoS attacks and take preventive measures.

— Safety sensor data

Security sensors deployed in the 4G/LTE network can provide additional data on malicious activity, such as intrusion attempts, port scans, abnormal application behavior and so on. This data is usually collected using intrusion detection systems (IDS) or intrusion prevention systems (IPS), which continuously monitor network traffic for suspicious behavior.

Combining these different data sources provides a comprehensive overview of the 4G/LTE network, facilitating early detection of DDoS attacks and appropriate corrective action.

2.2.2   Data pre-processing techniques

Before applying DDoS attack detection algorithms, it is essential to pre-process the collected data in order to improve its quality and reduce potential errors. Data pre-processing techniques play a crucial role in this process, preparing data for more effective analysis.

— *Data normalization:* data normalization is the technique of scaling data to a common range, often between 0 and 1, or using the standard distribution. This ensures that the different characteristics of the data have an equal influence on the machine learning algorithms, and prevents certain characteristics from dominating others.

— *Dimension reduction:* the aim of dimension reduction is to reduce the number of features or variables in a data set, while preserving as much of the important information as possible. This technique can be carried out using methods such as principal component analysis (PCA) or feature selection. By reducing the dimensionality of data, DDoS attack detection models can be simplified and their computational efficiency improved.

— *Noise and outlier elimination:* the aim of noise and outlier elimination is to remove irrelevant or incorrect data that could distort the results of the analysis. This can be achieved by using smoothing, filtering or thresholding techniques to identify and remove outliers or random fluctuations that are not representative of normal network behavior.

By combining these data pre-processing techniques, it is possible to improve data quality and efficiently prepare data for accurate analysis of DDoS attack detection in 4G/LTE networks.

2.3. DDoS attack detection models for 4G/LTE networks

The following section explores DDoS attack detection models specifically designed for 4G/LTE networks. Before diving into the details, a taxonomy of the different machine learning (ML) and deep learning (DL) models used, as well as their respective performances, is presented in Table II.1.

References	ML/DL models	Applications	Accuracy
[36] [37, 38]	CNN NB, KNN, DT, SVM, RF, LR	Image Processing Miscellaneous	99% 99% (DT, RF)
[39]	ANN	Miscellaneous	99.95%
[40] [41]	LoR, NB RF	Miscellaneous K-fold	99-100% (LoR)[5] 99.885%
[30, 42-46]	RNN	Gradient Descent	99.9%
[45] [43]	RF, NN RNN, LSTM, Bi-LSTM, GRU	Miscellaneous Miscellaneous	95.2% (RF) Best with RNN [10]
[47]	LBDMIDS	Miscellaneous	Best Performance
[48]	ANN	Miscellaneous	99%
[49] [50]	Shallow NN SVM, MLP, LSTM, BiLSTM, LDA, KNN, RF	Backpropagation Miscellaneous	Good Best with BiLSTM
[44]	RNN ELM	Linear Regression	Up to 99
[51]	LSTM	-	97.37%
[52]	LSTM	Binary Classification	99%
[53]	CNN-BiLSTM	Combination	99.76%

Table II.1 - Taxonomy of ML/DL Models for DDoS Attack Detection

2.3.1 Machine Learning (ML) models

Machine Learning (ML) models offer a promising approach to detecting DDoS attacks in 4G/LTE networks. These models are capable of learning from collected data and detecting abnormal patterns and behaviors associated with DDoS attacks.

— *K nearest neighbors (KNN)* [37, 38]: the k nearest neighbors (KNN) model is a classification method that assigns a label to a data point based on the labels of neighboring data points in feature space. In the context of DDoS attack detection, KNN can be used to classify network traffic according to its characteristics, identifying anomalies that do not correspond to normal traffic patterns.

— *Support vector machines (SVMs)* [50]: Support vector machines (SVMs) are supervised learning models used for classification and regression. In DDoS attack detection, SVMs can be trained to distinguish normal traffic patterns from abnormal patterns associated with DDoS attacks. SVMs are efficient at handling high-dimensional data sets and are able

30

to generalize from non-linear data.

— *Decision trees (DT)*: Decision trees are supervised learning models that use a tree structure to represent and classify data. They are easy to interpret and understand, making them attractive for detecting DDoS attacks in 4G/LTE networks. Decision trees can be used to identify important characteristics of network traffic and to make detection decisions based on these characteristics.

Using these Machine Learning models, it is possible to build efficient and accurate DDoS attack detection systems for 4G/LTE networks, enabling wireless communication services to be protected against security threats.

2.3.2   Deep Learning (DL) models

Deep Learning models offer a powerful approach to detecting DDoS attacks in 4G/LTE networks by enabling complex representations to be learned from raw data. Among the most commonly used Deep Learning techniques are :

— *Deep neural networks*: deep neural networks, such as *convolutional neural networks (CNNs) and recurrent neural networks (RNNs)*, are capable of learning hierarchical representations from structured or unstructured data. In the context of DDoS attack detection, CNNs can be used to extract relevant features from network traffic flows, while RNNs can be used to model temporal sequences of traffic and detect anomalous behavior associated with DDoS attacks.

- *Recurrent neural networks for temporal sequence detection*: recurrent neural networks (RNNs) are particularly well suited to modeling temporal sequences, such as network traffic sequences in 4G/LTE networks. RNNs can be used to detect anomalous temporal patterns associated with DDoS attacks, by analyzing traffic dynamics and trends over time.

Several studies [36, 37, 39, 48, 49, 51-53] focus on the use of *recurrent neural networks (RNNs)* and *long short-term memories (LSTMs)* for DDoS attack detection, with promising results. In addition, hybrid models, approaches based on *extreme machine learning (ELM) algorithms* and feature extraction techniques are also explored.

2.4. Model performance evaluation

In this section, we look in detail at the metrics and methods used to evaluate the effectiveness of DDoS attack detection models in 4G/LTE networks. We also discuss the experimental results obtained from different evaluation techniques.

2.4.1 Evaluation metrics

Evaluating the performance of DDoS attack detection models in 4G/LTE networks requires the use of appropriate metrics to measure model effectiveness and reliability. Among the most commonly used evaluation metrics are :

To assess the performance of the models used in our study, several metrics are used, including the confusion matrix. This matrix comprises four metrics: *True Positive (TP)*, *True Negative (TN)*, *False Positive (FP)* and *False Negative (FN)*. The *Accuracy* metric shows how often trained models correctly detect desired attacks. It is calculated using the following formula:

$$\text{Accuracy} = \frac{TP + TN}{TP + TN + FP + FN} \tag{II.1}$$

Precision defines the model's performance, indicating the TPs suggested by the classifier. It is calculated using the following expression :

$$\text{Precision} = \frac{TP}{TP + FP} \tag{II.2}$$

Precision is an important measure of the model's ability to correctly identify true positives among all positive predictions. High precision indicates that the model is less likely to misclassify negative samples as positive. However, it is important to note that accuracy alone does not provide a complete picture of model performance, and it must be interpreted in conjunction with other measures such as *'Recall'* and *'Fl-score'* for a more complete assessment.

The model *"Recall"* is calculated using equation (II.3).

$$\text{Recall} = \frac{TP}{TP + FN} \tag{II.3}$$

The "F1 score" is considered a better evaluation parameter, as it combines both accuracy and "Recall". We can find the model's "F1 score "1 using equation (II.4).

$$\text{F1 score} = 2 \times \frac{(\text{Precision} \times \text{Recall})}{(\text{Precision} + \text{Recall})} \tag{II.4}$$

2.4.2 Case study and experimental results

As part of the performance evaluation of DDoS attack detection models in 4G/LTE networks, experiments were carried out on real datasets. For this evaluation, the CIC-DDoS2019 dataset [54] was used because of its diversity, providing a set of DDoS attacks. The use of this dataset [54] made it possible to evaluate the effectiveness of DDoS attack detection methods in contexts other than 4G/LTE mobile networks, by testing different detection techniques using the network flow characteristics provided by the dataset. This approach made it possible to evaluate the models' ability to detect and respond to attacks, and to compare their respective performances. Models based on machine learning and deep learning demonstrated adaptability by learning from the data and adjusting to new traffic patterns without the need for constant manual updates. In addition, these models offered high performance in terms of precision, recall and ability to generalize from non-linear or complex data, making them particularly effective in detecting sophisticated and emerging DDoS attacks.

However, it's important to note some of the drawbacks of machine learning and deep learning-based approaches, including the need for labeled data for model training, as well as the computational complexity associated with these approaches.

These considerations need to be taken into account when choosing a method for detecting DDoS attacks in 4G/LTE networks, depending on the specific needs of the organization, the availability of resources and the nature of the attacks it faces.

Conclusion

To conclude this chapter on techniques for detecting DDoS attacks in 4G/LTE networks, it's clear that both traditional approaches and machine learning (ML/DL)-based methods offer solutions, but with distinct advantages and limitations.

Traditional approaches, such as signature-based filtering and behavioral analysis, are well established and have proven their effectiveness in many cases. They offer robust detection of DDoS attacks by focusing on predefined rules and detection thresholds. However, they can be limited in terms of their ability to detect new forms of attack or to handle very high traffic loads.

On the other hand, *machine learning-based* techniques such as *deep neural networks* and *machine learning (ML) models* offer a more flexible and adaptive approach to DDoS attack detection. These models can learn from raw data and detect complex patterns associated with DDoS attacks, making them particularly effective in detecting sophisticated and evolving attacks.

Chapter 3: Case study of DDoS detection on a 4G/LTE network

In this chapter, we will look at an in-depth study of a real case of DDoS detection in a 4G/LTE network, using the CIC-DDoS2019 dataset [54]as the main reference for analyzing attacks and exploring effective detection methods.

3.1. Introduction to case studies with the CIC- dataset DDoS2019

The introduction to the case study with the CIC-DDoS2019 dataset [54] provides an essential overview of the approach taken to analyze DDoS attacks in 4G/LTE networks. By highlighting the design and objectives of this dataset, this section establishes a relevant framework for the in-depth analysis that follows.

3.1.1 CIC-DDoS2019 dataset presentation [54]

The CIC-DDoS2019 dataset has been designed to offer a holistic perspective on DDoS attacks by providing a variety of data relevant to the analysis and detection of these attacks in 4G/LTE networks. Here are some details on the origins and features of this dataset:

- Dataset origin: The dataset was created by the Canadian Institute for Cybersecurity (CIC), a cybersecurity research center affiliated to the University of New Brunswick in Canada. It was developed as part of research projects aimed at better understanding and improving the detection of DDoS attacks.

— Dataset composition: The CIC-DDoS2019 dataset is composed of network traffic data generated by DDoS attack simulation scenarios. These scenarios include a variety of DDoS attack types, such as UDP Flood, TCP Flood, HTTP Flood and so on. Data is organized into records or streams, each representing a sequence of packets or events on the network.

— Data characteristics : Dataset data includes a range of characteristics relevant to DDoS attack analysis. This can include information such as: Network traffic characteristics, such as source and destination IP addresses, ports used, transport protocols, etc. Network performance metrics, such as bandwidth, delay, jitter, etc. Specific DDoS attack markers or indicators, such as abnormal traffic patterns, sudden variations in network load, etc. Metadata on simulated attacks, such as attack type, intensity, duration, etc.

— Variety of simulated attacks: The dataset includes a variety of simulated DDoS attacks, making it a valuable resource for assessing the robustness of detection systems. These attacks can be of various types, including:

  - UDP Flood: Massive sending of UDP packets to overwhelm processing capacity.
  - TCP Flood: Similar to UDP Flood, but uses TCP to saturate resources.
  - HTTP Flood: Massive sending of HTTP requests to make a web server unavailable.
  - Other types: May include ICMP Flood, SYN Flood, etc.

— Network traffic data - Dataset records provide :

  - Packet information (IP/TCP/UDP headers, payload data, etc.).
  - Flow characteristics (duration, number and size of packets, etc.).
  - Aggregated traffic statistics (bandwidth, total number of packets, etc.).

— Attack annotations: In the dataset, each record is annotated to indicate whether it belongs to a DDoS attack.

— Scalability and realism: The dataset is designed to be scalable and to represent realistic scenarios, enabling testing under a variety of conditions.

By combining these aspects, the CIC-DDoS2019 dataset provides a solid foundation for DDoS attack detection research, enabling new detection techniques to be explored, the performance of existing models to be assessed, and contributions to be made to improving the security of 4G/LTE networks.

3.1.2   Study objectives and use of the dataset

We define the objectives of our study, which are to analyze DDoS attacks on 4G/LTE networks using the CIC-DDoS2019 dataset as our main reference point.

We use the CIC-DDoS2019 dataset [54] to detect DDoS attacks on 4G/LTE mobile networks for the several reasons:

— The CIC-DDoS2019 dataset [54] is specifically designed for the study of DDoS attacks, making it particularly relevant to our study, which focuses on the detection of this type of attack in 4G/LTE mobile networks.

— Another reason is that the CIC-DDoS2019 dataset [54] contains examples of real DDoS attacks, enabling us to analyze and detect different types of such attacks, including those that may specifically target 4G/LTE mobile networks, in the absence of datasets from one or more 4G/LTE mobile networks.

— We also note that the CIC-DDoS2019 dataset [54] is relatively large and contains a diversity of DDoS attacks simulated in various environments. This allows us to have a representative dataset to train and evaluate detection models.

— Not least because the CIC-DDoS2019 dataset [54] has become a benchmark in the cybersecurity community for DDoS attack detection research.

The main objective of our study is to analyze DDoS attacks in 4G/LTE networks. This analysis includes several aspects, such as identifying the most common types of attack, understanding the traffic patterns associated with these attacks, assessing the impact of attacks on network performance, etc. By better understanding the characteristics and consequences of DDoS attacks in 4G/LTE networks, we will be able to help strengthen the resilience of these networks against such threats.

— Using datasets to analyze DDoS attacks on 4G/LTE networks

We have chosen the CIC-DDoS2019 dataset as the main reference point for your analysis. This dataset offers a variety of data relevant to the study of DDoS attacks, including in the specific context of 4G/LTE networks. Using this dataset, we can: Identify traffic patterns associated with DDoS attacks in 4G/LTE networks. Evaluate the effectiveness of existing attack detection techniques in this context. Develop new detection methods specifically adapted to the characteristics of 4G/LTE networks. Examine the impact of DDoS attacks on 4G/LTE network performance, such as latency, bandwidth, quality of service, etc. Provide valuable insights for 4G/LTE network operators and security providers to strengthen protection against DDoS attacks.

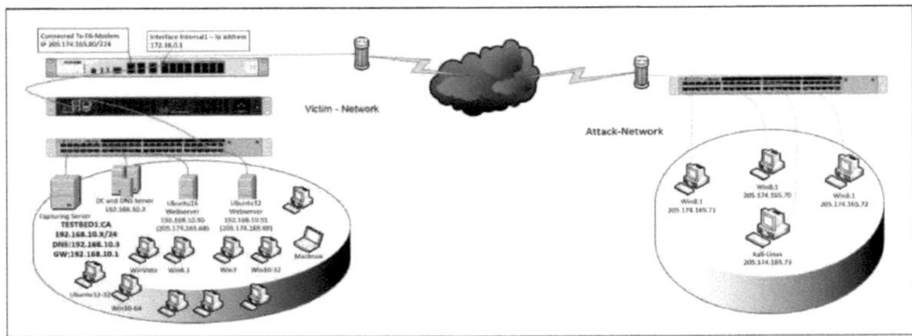

FIGURE III.1 - Architecture of the CIC-DDoS2019 dataset construction testbed [54].

The main priority in building this dataset [54] was to generate realistic background traffic. The authors used a *B-Profile system*[36] proposed in [55] to profile the abstract behavior of human interactions and generate naturalistic benign background traffic in the testbed proposed in Figure III.1. For this dataset integrates the abstract behavior of 25 users based on *HTTP, HTTPS, FTP,*

---

36 *The B-Profile system* refers to a *Quality of Service (QoS)* profile defined for data transfer in the network. This profile can specify various parameters related to bandwidth, latency, reliability and other aspects of data transmission. It is used to guarantee a certain quality of service for the various applications and services running on the network, according to their specific performance requirements.

3.2. Analysis of DDoS attack characteristics on 4G/LTE networks

3.2.1 Types of DDoS attacks present in the dataset

The CIC-DDoS2019 dataset [54] contains different types of modern DDoS attacks such as *PortMap, NetBIOS, LDAP, MSSQL, UDP, UDP-Lag, SYN, NTP, DNS and SNMP.* The attacks were executed over a period of time. As shown in Table III.1, 12 DDoS attacks including *NTP, DNS, LDAP, MSSQL, NetBIOS, SNMP, SSDP, UDP, UDP-Lag, WebDDoS, SYN and TFTP* (see Table III.2) were executed on the training day and 7 attacks including *PortScan, NetBIOS, LDAP, MSSQL, UDP, UDP-Lag and SYN* (see Table III.2) were executed on the test day. The volume of traffic for *WebDDoS*[37] was very low and PortScan was run only on the test day, and is used as model test data.

---

37 *WebDDoS* is a DDoS attack targeting web applications.

Days	Attacks	Attack Time
First Day	PortMap	9:43 - 9:51
	NetBIOS	10:00 - 10:09
	LDAP	10:21 - 10:30
	MSSQL	10:33 - 10:42
	UDP	10:53 - 11:03
	UDP-Lag	11:14 - 11:24
	SYN	11:28 - 17:35
Second Day	NTP	10:35 - 10:45
	DNS	10:52 - 11:05
	LDAP	11:22 - 11:32
	MSSQL	11:36 - 11:45
	NetBIOS	11:50 - 12:00
	SNMP	12:12 - 12:23
	SSDP	12:27 - 12:37
	UDP	12:45 - 13:09
	UDP-Lag	13:11 - 13:15
	WebDDoS	13:18 - 13:29
	SYN	13:29 - 13:34
	TFTP	13:35 - 17:15

TABLE III.1 - Table of attacks by day and attack time

DDoS ATTACK TYPE	
NTP (NETWORK TIME PROTO- COL)	THE ATTACK USES AMPLIFIED NTP REQUESTS TO OVERWHELM THE TARGET.
DNS (DOMAIN NAME SYS- TEM)	THE ATTACK EXPLOITS DNS QUERIES TO SATURATE TARGET DNS SERVERS.
LDAP (LIGHTWEIGHT DIREC- TORY ACCESS PROTOCOL)	THE ATTACK AIMS TO EXHAUST LDAP SERVER RESOURCES.
MSSQL (MICROSOFT SQL SER- VER)	THE ATTACK TARGETS MICROSOFT SQL SERVERS WITH MALICIOUS QUERIES.
NETBIOS (NETWORK BIOS)	THE ATTACK USES NETBIOS REQUESTS TO SATURATE THE TARGET NETWORK.
SNMP (SIMPLE NETWORK MA- NAGEMENT PROTOCOL)	THE ATTACK EXPLOITS SNMP REQUESTS TO OVERLOAD NETWORK EQUIPMENT.
SSDP (SIMPLE SERVICE DISCO- VERY PROTOCOL)	THE ATTACK AIMS TO OVERWHELM DEVICES USING SSDP WITH MALICIOUS REQUESTS.
UDP (USER DATAGRAM PROTO- COL)	THE ATTACK AIMS TO FLOOD THE TARGET WITH UDP PACKETS, OFTEN USED IN VOLUMETRIC DDoS ATTACKS.
UDP-LAG	THE ATTACK AIMS TO REDUCE PERFORMANCE BY FRAGMENTING AND ASYNCHRONOUSLY SENDING UDP PACKETS.
WEBDDOS	DISTRIBUTED DENIAL OF SERVICE (DDoS) ATTACK TARGETING WEB APPLICATIONS TO SATURATE SERVER RESOURCES.
SYN (SYNCHRONIZE)	THE SYN FLOOD ATTACK EXPLOITS THE TCP PROTOCOL TO SATURATE THE RESOURCES OF THE TARGET SERVER.
TFTP (TRIVIAL FILE TRANSFER PROTOCOL)	THE ATTACK AIMS TO EXHAUST TFTP SERVER RESOURCES WITH FICHIER TRANSFER REQUESTS.

TABLE III.2 - Types of DDoS attacks in the CIC-DDoS2019 dataset [54].

3.2. The specifics and limitations of the CIC-DDoS2019 dataset in the analysis of DDoS attacks in 4G/LTE networks

In this section, we explore the distinctive features of the CIC-DDoS2019 dataset in the context of analyzing DDoS attacks on 4G/LTE networks, while identifying its specific features as well as its limitations. This analysis will provide a better understanding of the relevance and challenges associated with using this dataset to detect DDoS attacks in the specific context of 4G/LTE mobile networks.

3.3.1 Specificities of the CIC-DDoS2019 dataset in the analysis of DDoS attacks in 4G/LTE networks

In this section, we propose to examine the distinctive features of the CIC-DDoS2019 dataset [54] and their impact on the analysis of DDoS attacks in 4G/LTE networks. To this end, we propose in Table III.3 a classification of DDoS attacks in 4G/LTE networks present in the CIC-DDoS2019 dataset [54].

The classification proposed by Table III.3 aims to identify the different categories of DDoS attacks present in the CIC-DDoS2019 dataset [54] that can target the specific components and protocols of 4G/LTE networks, as well as the direct consequences on the services and critical resources of these networks. This proves once again that the CIC-DDoS2019 dataset [54] is a valuable resource for the analysis of DDoS attacks in 4G/LTE networks, offering a variety of scenarios and real data for security research.

3.3.2 The limits of dataset CIC-DDoS2019 in the analysis of DDoS attacks in 4G/LTE networks

Despite its advantages, the CIC-DDoS2019 dataset [54] also has some limitations to consider when using it. Firstly, although the attack scenarios are diverse, they may not represent the full range of potential attacks in a real LTE network. Consequently, the results obtained from this dataset may not be fully generalizable to all situations. Furthermore, as with any dataset, the quality of the data and the representativeness of the scenarios must be carefully assessed to ensure the validity of the conclusions drawn from the analysis. In addition, the data collection conditions and simulation methods used to generate the attacks in the dataset may not be entirely generalizable to all situations.

4G/LTE DDoS attacks	DDoS attacks present in the CIC-DDoS2019 dataset [54]
BOTNET-lAUNCHED DDoS ATTACKS *(NETWORK ACCESS)*	NTP (NTP amplification attack) DNS (DNS amplification attack) LDAP (LDAP amplification attack) MSSQL (MSSQL amplification attack) NetBIOS (NetBIOS amplification attack) SNMP (SNMP amplification attack) SSDP (SSDP amplification attack)
OVERLOAD OF HSS *(CORE NETWORK)*	LDAP (LDAP amplification attack) MSSQL (MSSQL amplification attack)
OVERLOAD OF SGW *(CORE NETWORK)*	WEBDDoS (DDoS attack on web services) SYN DDoS (SYN flooding attack) TFTP DDoS (TFTP amplification attack) UDP-Lag (excessive use of UDP resulting in latency) UDP DDoS (UDP flooding attack)

TABLE III.3 - Classification of 4G/LTE DDoS attacks present in the CIC- DDoS2019 dataset [54].

not always accurately reflect the real-life conditions of an LTE network under stress or attack.

3.4. Approach based on RNN, LSTM and GRU models for detection and classification

In this chapter, an approach based on the RNN model [45, 46] is proposed for detecting DDoS attacks. In addition, the RNN, LSTM and GRU models [XXX] are used for binary and multi-class classification. The methodology adopted in this study, illustrated in Figure III.2, comprises several steps such as data normalization, feature extraction, model training and attack detection modules.

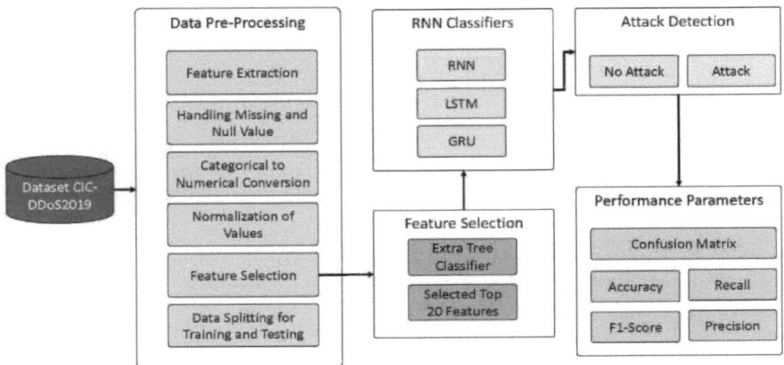

FIGURE III.2 - The methodology adopted in our study.

Figure III.2 shows that the CIC-DDoS2019 dataset [54] is used for the experiments. In order to optimize model performance, the dataset undergoes textsl(Data Pre-Processing) in several stages. Missing and null values are eliminated to reduce data ambiguity and improve the model training process. *Categorical values* are converted to numerical values according to the needs of the deep learning models. Next, the data is normalized. During this stage, a feature selection is performed to choose the 20 best features. This selection is aimed at achieving better model performance with *lower computational complexity.*[3]

less. The selected features are the most effective for detecting DDoS attacks in network traffic. Finally, the data is divided into training and test subsets to train the RNN, LSTM and GRU models for binary and multi-class attack classification. The test subset is then used to evaluate the performance of the trained models.

3.4.1 *Data Preprocessing*

Before training the model, the dataset must be pre-processed to eliminate noise and reduce the amount of redundant or unnecessary data. Data pre-processing is necessary to improve model performance and reduce computational complexity.

— *Standard scalar normalization*: the CIC-DDoS2019 dataset [54] contains different features with different dimensions, scales and distributions. For example, the 'Fwd Packets/s' feature contains very large values for some records, while very small ones for others. Using these raw features to train DL models tends to show poor performance. Standard scalar normalization will ensure that features are scaled and that no individual feature has a disproportionate impact on the results. This preserves the relationship between minimum and maximum values for each feature.

— *Dealing with missing and null values (Dealing with Categorical Values)*: Dealing with missing and null values is an important step in data pre-processing that can have an impact on model accuracy and precision. This phase removes missing or null values from the dataset. Removing these records reduces computational complexity and improves model performance [56].

— *Dealing with Categorical Values*: this phase converts categorical values into numerical values, as ML/DL models work on numerical values. We use label coding and one-hot coding methods to convert categorical data types into numerical data types. In our study, we used *the sklearn library*[38] [39] which provides a tool called *LabelEncoder*[40] used to transform categorical data into numerical data [57].

— *Feature Selection*: This step is important in data preprocessing. By selecting important, weighted features from the CICDDoS2019 dataset [54], the model's attack prediction can be increased. *A decision tree-based classifier*[41] is used for feature selection. It selects the top features using the decision tree approach. For this study, the 20 best features are selected *('Timestamp' , 'Source Port', 'Min Packet Length', 'Fwd Packet Length Min ', 'Flow ID ', 'Packet Length Mean ', 'Fwd Packet Length Max', 'Average Packet Size ', 'ACK Flag*

---

to run an algorithm or solve a problem.

39 The *scikit-learn* library, often abbreviated to sklearn, is one of Python's machine learning libraries. It offers a wide range of tools for classification, regression, clustering, dimensionality reduction, model selection and much more.

40 *LabelEncoder* is an ML utility class used to encode categorical labels into numerical values. It is commonly used to convert non-numerical labels (e.g. text categories) into numerical representations that can be fed into ML algorithms.

41 *Decision tree-based classifiers* are a type of supervised learning algorithm used for classification tasks, whose aim is to predict the class label of input data based on the values of its features.

Count', 'Avg Fwd Segment Size ', 'Fwd Packet Length Mean ', 'Flow Bytess', 'Max Packet Length ', 'Protocol', 'Fwd Packetss', 'Flow Packetss', 'Total Length of Fwd Packets', 'Subflow Fwd Bytes', 'Destination Port', and 'act_data_pkt_fwd') using an additional tree classifier. The selected features are used for model training in our study.

— *Data splitting*: Data splitting is a crucial step in data preparation [58]. The CIC-DDoS2019 dataset [54] is split into training and test sets. The Sklearn library is used for data splitting [59]. In total, 70% of the data is used for training and 30% for testing.

3.4.2 The classification models used

This study uses *RNN (Recurrent Neural Networks), GRU (Gated Recurrent Unit) and LSTM (Long Short-Term Memory)* models to detect DDoS attacks. A brief presentation of these models follows.

We have chosen *RNNs, GRUs and LSTMs* in our study for their effectiveness in detecting DDoS attacks. Firstly, according to the literature review [45, 46], *RNNs* are renowned for their ability to process data sequences, which is particularly relevant in the context of DDoS attack detection, where network traffic data is often sequential and time-dependent.

Then, more advanced variants of *RNNs*, such as *LSTMs* [45] and *GRUs* [60-62], were chosen to overcome the problem of the gradient disappearing when learning long sequences. In the case of DDoS attacks, where patterns can be complex and interact over multiple time scales, the use of models such as LSTMs and GRUs can effectively capture these complex temporal relationships.

In addition, the study is based on a large dataset, the CIC-DDoS2019 dataset [54], which contains a large amount of network traffic data. The *RNN, GRU and LSTM* models are known to work well with large amounts of data, making them suitable choices for our study where large-scale data analysis is required for accurate detection of DDoS attacks.

Finally, the selection of these models also aligns with best practice in DDoS attack detection [55, 63], where the use of deep learning-based models such as RNN, GRU and LSTM is common due to their ability to capture complex patterns in network traffic data.

3.4.3   Recurrent Neural Networks (RNN)

RNN models have many applications, including image processing, market prediction, handwriting recognition and speech recognition. RNNs work best on large amounts of data, and the use of backpropagation improves its final result. *The gradient vanishing problem in backpropagation*[42] occurs in RNN and is handled by its variants the LSTM and GRU models. The RNN model is adopted in our study because the data set is large and contains sequences of attacks.

3.4.4   The LSTM (Long Short-Term Memory) model

We also chose LSTM for the analysis of network traffic data for its ability to remember previous entries, enabling us to find patterns and enduring connections in the input sequences. The CIC-DDoS2019 dataset [54] contains attack details such as flow lengths, source and destination IP addresses, and port number, demonstrating the sequential nature of attacks in network traffic. LSTM also overcomes the missing gradient problem of RNNs. In addition, it is used in real-world applications where data is voluminous and data manipulation is more complicated. LSTM works by means of an input/output/forget gate, which controls the flow of attacks into and out of cells. Attacks are memorized by the LSTM cell. The LSTM model is trained to classify instances as normal or attacking. It has the ability to detect patterns in regular network traffic to detect DDoS attacks. For multi-classification, network traffic instance values are set to 0, 1, 2, 3. For model training, we used each instance type from the network traffic training dataset for appropriate attack type detection. Label coding is used to label all attack types and convert the attack into a specific value. The memory cell function of the LSTM model successfully categorizes network traffic attacks.

3.4.5   The GRU (Gated Recurrent Unit) model

In our study, we also chose to use the GRU model to detect attacks in network traffic, as it requires less memory and is more time-efficient. It captures long-term relationships in the temporal flow of network traffic. Compared with RNN and LSTM models, the GRU model is easier to use, increasing computational efficiency without compromising its ability to accurately predict the temporal dynamics of data. It requires less training time because it has a simplified gate arrangement with no output gates. The GRU model operates with two sigmoid gates and a hidden state. It has the ability to find patterns in regular network traffic to detect DDOS attacks from the CIC-DDoS2019 dataset [54].

---

42 *The backpropagation vanishing gradient problem* refers to a challenge encountered when training deep neural networks using the backpropagation algorithm. Backpropagation is the process of updating the weights of a neural network to minimize the difference between predicted and actual output, usually using gradient descent or its variants.

PARAMETERS	RNN	LSTM	GRU
ACTIVATOR	RELU, SOFTMAX (MULTICLASS), SIGMOID (BINARY CLASS)	RELU, SOFTMAX (MULTICLASS), SIGMOID (BINARY CLASS)	RELU, SOFTMAX (MULTICLASS), SIGMOID (BINARY CLASS)
OPTIMIZER	ADAM	ADAM	ADAM
LEARNING RATE	0.001	0.001	0.001
LOSS	CATEGORICAL CROSS ENTROPY (MULTICLASS), BINARY CROSS ENTROPY (BINARY-CLASS)	CATEGORICAL CROSS ENTROPY (MULTICLASS), BINARY CROSS ENTROPY (BINARY-CLASS)	CATEGORICAL CROSS ENTROPY (MULTICLASS), BINARY CROSS ENTROPY (BINARY-CLASS)
RNN/LSTM/GRU LAYERS	2	2	2
HIDDEN LAYERS	2	2	2
NEURONS PER LSTM LAYERS	8	8	8
NEURONS PER HIDDEN LAYERS	16, 8 (1ST LAYER, 2ND LAYER)	16, 8 (1ST LAYER, 2ND LAYER)	16, 8 (1ST LAYER, 2ND LAYER)
BATCH SIZE	1000	1000	1000
EPOCHS	100	100	100

TABLE III.4 - RNN, LSTM and GRU model parameters

3.4.6 RNN parameters used

In our RNN models, we use the linear rectified activation function *(ReLU)*. By applying the ReLU function, the models learn the complex characteristics of the network's hidden layers. Compared with other activation functions such as *sigmoid and tanh,* ReLU results are more efficient. For optimization, the *Adam*[43] algorithm is used. It combines the *RMSprop (Root Mean Square Propagation)*[44] and *AdaGrad (Adaptive Gradient Algorithm)*[45] techniques, modifying the latter according to the first and second moments of the gradients, thus preserving the pre-parameterized learning rates. The Adam optimizer dynamically adjusts the learning rate for each parameter during training, effectively updating the weights of the LSTM and GRU models.

3.5. Assessment of DDoS attack detection

In this section, we take a detailed look at the performance and results of DDoS attack

---

43 *The Adam algorithm* is the optimization method used in training recurrent neural networks (RNNs) as well as other types of neural networks, such as Convolutional Neural Networks (CNNs) and Fully Connected Neural Networks (FCNs).

44 *RMSprop (Root Mean Square Propagation)* is an adaptive method that adjusts learning rates individually for each network parameter based on gradient history.

45 *AdaGrad (Adaptive Gradient Algorithm)* is an optimization algorithm commonly used in neural network training, including recurrent neural networks (RNN). Its aim is to adapt the learning rate adaptively for each model parameter, based on the gradient history observed for that parameter.

detection techniques using the CIC-DDoS2019 dataset [54].

3.5.1 Implementation of RNN models

This study used the *RNN* [45, 46], *LSTM* [30, 45] and *GRU* [60-62, 64] models for DDoS attack identification using the CICDDOS2019 dataset, publicly available at [54]. The selected dataset contains thousands of DDoS attacks divided into 12 classes, including *DNS, SNMP, NTP, WebDDoS, MSSQL, UDP, LDAP, NetBIOS, SSDP, PortScan, UDP-Lag and SYN.* This study performs both binary and multi-class classification involving all 12 classes. For all twelve attacks, plans were implemented on the training day, and seven attacks were executed on the test day; attacks against *DNS, SNMP, NTP, WebDDoS, MSSQL, UDP, LDAP, UDP-Lag, NetBIOS, SSDP, SYN and TFTP* were part of the training day, while attacks against *LDAP, PortScan, MSSQL, UDP-Lag, UDP and SYN* were part of the test day.

3.5.2   The experimental configuration

In this study, we implemented our models using the Python programming language. A Jupyter Notebook was used to run the experiment. The deep learning (DL) application API libraries pandas, matplotlib, sci-kit-learn, Keras and scipy were used to implement the DL models.

Experiments are conducted using the CIC-DDoS2019 dataset [54] for binary and multi-class classification. The results obtained are evaluated in terms of *Precision, Recall Accuracy, F1-score* and confusion matrix for each attack detection model. These measures are used to evaluate the performance of the models in detecting DDoS attacks. These evaluations provide an in-depth understanding of the effectiveness of the proposed DDoS attack detection methods and their ability to generalize on the CIC- DDoS2019 dataset [54].

3.5.3   Binary classification

The CICDDoS2019 dataset [54] offers very interesting results in DDoS detection by binary classification using the *RNN, LSTM and GRU* models, as shown in Figure III.3. LSTM and GRU performed well in intrusion detection on the CIC-DDOS2019 dataset [54]. They demonstrated good accuracy, good "Recall" and a good "F1-score", suggesting their usefulness for detecting and categorizing cyberthreats. In terms of execution time, GRU outperformed LSTM, with a much lower execution time of 59.875 [s] compared with 96.25 [s] for LSTM and 750 [s] for RNN. The results suggest the computational efficiency of the GRU model while preserving performance. GRU's considerably fast execution time underlines its effectiveness as a real-time IDS solution.

Figure III.4 shows the validation and training *Accuracy* of the RNN, LSTM and GRU models. The blue line indicates the training accuracy *(Accuracy)* and the red line the validation accuracy

(Accuracy). Training *Accuracy* for the RNN model starts at 99.45% and reaches 99.99%. Model LSTM starts at 99.70% and reaches 99.9%, while validation *Accuracy* starts at 99.98% and reaches 99.99%. For the GRU model, training *Accuracy* starts at 98.4% and rises to 99.99%. This shows that the model is learning effectively from the training data and becoming more efficient in its predictions. As the model reaches its highest accuracy *(Accuracy)*, training accuracy *(Accuracy)* stabilizes, indicating that the model has successfully captured the underlying structure of the data and is producing consistent performance.

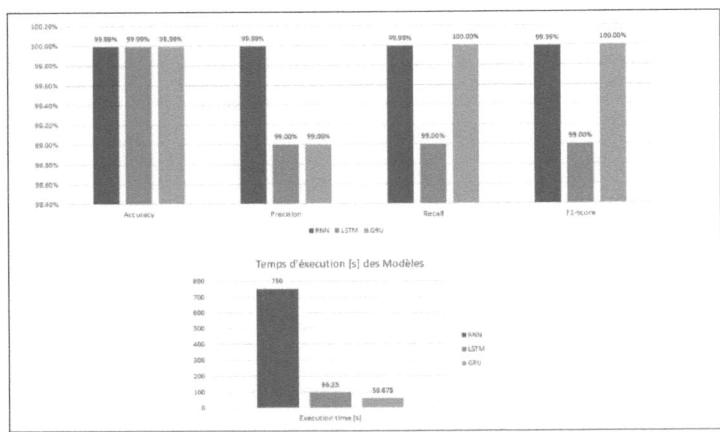

FIGURE III.3 - Model performance for DDoS detection using binary classification

3.5.4   Multi-class classification

In the context of multi-class classification, we can also note that the CIC-DDoS2019 dataset [54] offers very interesting results for DDoS detection based on *RNN, LSTM and GRU* models. The results are shown in Figure III.5. The *LSTM* and GRU models demonstrate a significant ability to distinguish between different classes of DDoS attacks. This ability is crucial in real-life environments where several types of attack can occur simultaneously. The results obtained indicate that these models are able to generalize effectively to different categories of attack, making them interesting for use in real-time attack detection systems. The high *Accuracy* and F1-scores achieved by the LSTM and GRU models testify to their effectiveness in the multi-class classification of DDoS attacks.

Figure III.6 illustrates the accuracy *(Accuracy)* of the RNN, LSTM and GRU models. Accuracy of the RNN model starts at 95.8% and reaches 99.15%. For the LSTM model, initial accuracy is 88%, rising to 99.9%. For the GRU model, initial accuracy is 83.25%, rising to 99.47%. These data indicate that the model is acquiring knowledge and improving its functionality over time.

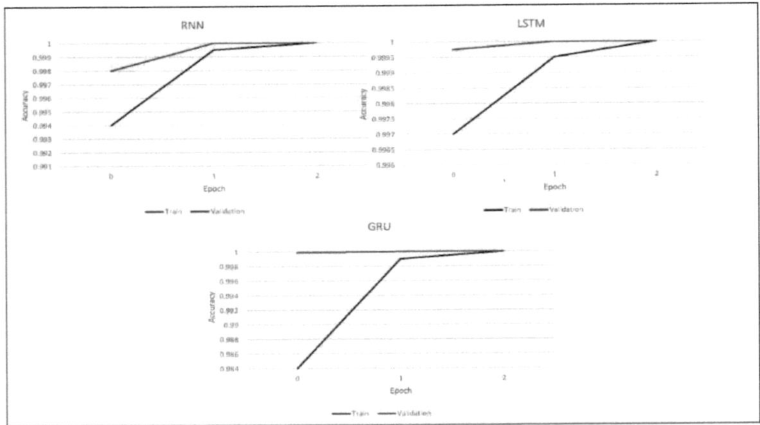

FIGURE III.4 - Model performance: Accuracy in DDoS detection by binary classification

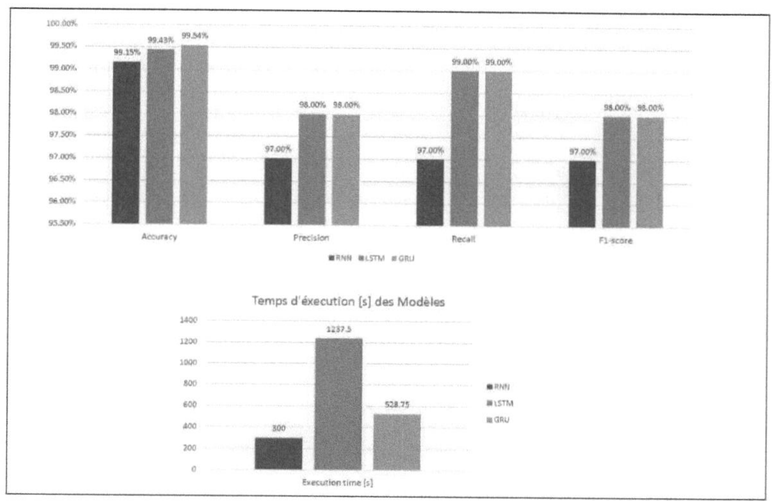

FIGURE III.5 - Model performance for DDoS detection using multi-class classification

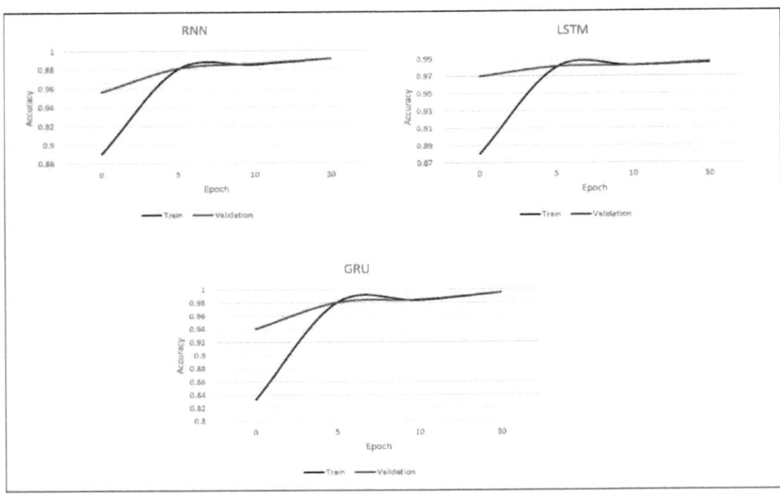

FIGURE III.6 - Model performance: Accuracy in DDoS detection using multi-class classification

3.5.4   Summary of results obtained

The results of our study show that the RNN, LSTM and GRU models perform very well in detecting DDoS attacks by binary and multi-class classification, using the CIC-DDoS2019 dataset. With regard to binary classification, LSTM and GRU perform well in terms of *Accuracy, Recall* and F1-score, suggesting their effectiveness in detecting DDoS attacks. suggesting their effectiveness in detecting and categorizing cyber threats. In addition, GRU stands out for its significantly lower execution time, underlining its effectiveness as a real-time IDS solution. For multi-class classification, LSTM and GRU demonstrate a significant ability to distinguish between different classes of attack, which is crucial in real-world environments. Their high performance in terms of accuracy and F1-score testifies to their effectiveness in this task. Furthermore, the results show that the models acquire knowledge and improve their functionality over time, reinforcing their usefulness in detecting DDoS attacks.

3.3.   Development of countermeasures for 4G/LTE network security

3.6.1   Proposed countermeasures to mitigate the impact of attacks

This section presents a series of strategies and techniques for countering DDoS attacks and reducing their impact on 4G/LTE networks. These measures are designed to reinforce the robustness of mobile communications infrastructures and ensure continuity of services for end users. Here are our recommendations:

Tables III.5 and III.6 summarize the various countermeasures we have proposed to mitigate the impact of DDoS attacks on 4G/LTE networks.

3.6.2   Recommendations for enhanced security in 4G/LTE networks

After proposing countermeasures to mitigate the impact of DDoS attacks on 4G/LTE networks, in this section we propose recommendations to enhance the security of 4G/LTE networks against DDoS attacks. Our aim is to propose practical guidelines for network operators to increase the robustness of their mobile communication infrastructures against such attacks.

INSTALLATION OF FILTERS AND FIREWALLS	DESCRIPTION
TRAFFIC FILTERING	TRAFFIC MONITORING AND ANALYSIS TO DETECT MALICIOUS ACTIVITY SUCH AS ABNORMAL TRAFFIC PATTERNS, SUSPICIOUS IP ADDRESSES, ETC.
FIREWALL POLICIES	TRAFFIC CONTROL BASED ON PREDEFINED SECURITY RULES TO BLOCK TRAFFIC FROM SPECIFIC IP ADDRESSES, COMMUNICATION PORTS, ETC.
EARLY DETECTION	CONFIGURE FILTERS AND FIREWALLS TO DETECT EARLY WARNING SIGNS OF AN IMPENDING ATTACK AND TAKE PREVENTIVE ACTION.
AUTOMATIC RESPONSE	INTEGRATION OF FILTERS AND FIREWALLS WITH AUTOMATED RESPONSE SYSTEMS TO AUTOMATICALLY BLOCK SUSPICIOUS TRAFFIC OR DIVERT IT TO SPECIALIZED MITIGATION CENTERS.

TABLE III.5 - Countermeasures: Installation of filters and firewalls

USE OF ANTI-DDOS CLOUD SERVICES	DESCRIPTION
DISTRIBUTED MITIGATION	REDIRECT SUSPICIOUS TRAFFIC TO CLOUD MITIGATION CENTERS TO REDUCE THE LOAD ON LOCAL INFRASTRUCTURES AND BENEFIT FROM HIGH FILTRATION AND MITIGATION CAPABILITIES.
REAL-TIME ANALYSIS	REAL-TIME ANALYSIS OF INCOMING TRAFFIC TO RAPIDLY DETECT AND MITIGATE DDOS ATTACKS USING ADVANCED ALGORITHMS AND MACHINE LEARNING TECHNIQUES.
SCALABILITY AND FLEXIBILITY	SCALABLE, FLEXIBLE MITIGATION CAPABILITY TO ADAPT TO FLUCTUATIONS IN DEMAND AND CHANGES IN THE THREAT LANDSCAPE.
REPORTING AND ANALYSIS	PROVIDE ADVANCED REPORTING AND ANALYSIS TOOLS TO MONITOR THE EFFECTIVENESS OF MITIGATION MEASURES AND ANALYZE TRENDS IN DDOS ATTACKS.

TABLE III.6 - Countermeasures: Use of Anti-DDoS Cloud Services

Guideline 1: Implement a global security strategy :

- Identify critical assets, vulnerabilities and threats specific to 4G/LTE networks, assessing the financial and operational impact of DDoS attacks.
- Define measurable objectives to guarantee protection against DDoS attacks, such as reducing detection time or improving mitigation capacity.
- Choose appropriate security solutions after identifying needs and risks, such as adopting advanced detection technologies or using anti-DDoS cloud services.
- Integrate security strategy with existing operational processes, involving teams from the outset and providing training on new security policies.
- Regularly evaluate and update the security strategy to take account of technological developments and lessons learned from previous incidents.

Guideline 2: Conduct regular risk assessments :

- Identify potential threats, including DDoS attacks, to understand attack scenarios and take preventive measures.

- Identify vulnerabilities in 4G/LTE infrastructures to correct them and strengthen security.
- Analyze the potential impact of DDoS attacks to quantify the financial and operational consequences and allocate resources appropriately.
- Prioritize corrective actions according to their severity and probability to enhance safety.

- Regularly monitor the effectiveness of mitigation measures and reassess risks to take account of changes in the threat environment.

Guideline 3: Strengthen staff training and awareness-raising

- Provide ongoing training on DDoS attack techniques and security best practices.
- Familiarize staff with emergency procedures for dealing with DDoS attacks.
- Raise staff awareness of good security practices to reduce the risk of DDoS attacks.
- Foster communication and collaboration between teams to detect, report and respond effectively to DDoS attacks.
- Encourage the sharing of knowledge and experience to strengthen the organization's resilience.

Guideline 4: Collaborate with other industry players

- Participate in threat information sharing initiatives to better understand trends in DDoS attacks.
- Exchange best safety practices to strengthen industry resilience.
- Working together to develop innovative safety solutions.
- Coordinate the response to DDoS attacks to minimize their impact on mobile communication services.

Guideline 5: Invest in advanced detection and mitigation technologies

- Use behavioral analysis technologies to detect DDoS attacks.
- Use machine learning techniques to improve detection of DDoS attacks.
- Use event correlation solutions to detect the warning signs of a DDoS attack.
- Use automatic mitigation technologies to mitigate the effects of DDoS attacks in real time.
- Implement real-time monitoring of network traffic for early detection of DDoS attacks.

Guideline 6: Establish incident management procedures

- Develop detailed DDoS incident management plans before an attack occurs.
- Identify and assess DDoS attacks to coordinate response.
- Notify internal and external stakeholders and ensure clear, transparent communication.
- Trigger mitigation measures to minimize the impact on mobile communication services.
- Monitor the evolution of the DDoS attack and evaluate the effectiveness of the mitigation measures implemented.
- Conduct a post-mortem analysis to identify gaps in the response and propose recommendations for improvement.

Conclusion

The case study presented offers an in-depth look at the detection of DDoS attacks in 4G/LTE networks, using the CIC-DDoS2019 dataset as the main reference point. Through our analysis, we were able to identify the different types of DDoS attacks present in the data, assess the effectiveness of existing detection techniques and explore the specificities as well as the limitations of the dataset in this context.

Our results highlight the crucial importance of developing detection methods specifically tailored to the characteristics of 4G/LTE networks, given the dynamic nature and QoS requirements of these networks. Furthermore, our study highlights the potential of the CIC-DDoS2019 dataset as a valuable resource for security research in the field of mobile networks.

However, it should be noted that despite the benefits of the CIC-DDoS2019 dataset, limitations remain, particularly with regard to the representativeness of attack scenarios and the fidelity of data collection conditions. Further efforts are therefore required to improve the quality and diversity of the data available for a more in-depth analysis of DDoS attacks in 4G/LTE networks.

General conclusion

Our in-depth study of DDoS attacks on 4G/LTE mobile networks has enabled us to highlight the growing complexity of these threats, and the crucial importance of effective detection in guaranteeing security and service availability. Through analysis of the theoretical underpinnings of attacks, 4G/LTE network security architectures and detection techniques, several significant conclusions have been drawn.

Firstly, it is clear that DDoS attacks represent a serious threat to 4G/LTE networks, due to their ability to coordinate large-scale attacks from multiple sources. The key characteristics of DDoS attacks, such as their scale, diversity and ability to morph, underline the need for proactive and adaptive detection to counter these threats.

Secondly, the security architecture of 4G/LTE networks offers robust defense mechanisms, but is not immune to DDoS attacks. Vulnerabilities in access networks, the core network, IMS and mobile equipment expose 4G/LTE networks to significant risks, requiring special attention to strengthen security measures.

Thirdly, both traditional and machine learning-based approaches offer solutions for detecting DDoS attacks in 4G/LTE networks. Traditional approaches, while proven, are limited in terms of their ability to detect new forms of attack, while machine learning-based techniques offer greater flexibility and adaptability, but require in-depth analysis of data and models.

Finally, the case study presented, using the CIC-DDoS2019 dataset [54], identified the different types of DDoS attacks, assessed the effectiveness of existing detection techniques and explored the specificities and limitations of the dataset in this context. The RNN, LSTM and GRU models proved highly effective in detecting DDoS attacks, with promising results for binary and multi-class classification.

Outlook

The study presented provides a solid basis for furthering the understanding and effectiveness of DDoS attack detection on 4G/LTE networks. In this section, we list some avenues that can be explored to further enrich this field:

(1) *Improving detection techniques:* Pursue research to develop new detection tech more robust and efficient detection techniques specifically adapted to the unique characteristics of 4G/LTE networks, taking into account the traffic patterns and bandwidth constraints of 4G/LTE. A study of hybrid models, approaches based on *extreme machine learning (ELM) algorithms* could be ebvisaged.

(2) *Validation on real-life scenarios:* Extend the study using real deployment scenarios to validate the effectiveness of detection techniques in operational environments that take into account load variations, network configurations and real attack behavior in 4G/LTE networks.

(3) *Industrial and academic collaboration:* Encourage collaboration between industrial players, telecoms service providers (mobile operators) and academic institutions to share data, best practices and research to strengthen the security of 4G/LTE networks against DDoS attacks.

(4) *Adapting to technological developments:* Anticipate and study the implications of technological developments such as the rollout of 5G on the detection and mitigation of DDoS attacks in mobile networks, identifying new threats and opportunities to strengthen network resilience.

REFERENCES

[1] Limei HE, Zheng YAN and Mohammed ATIQUZZAMAN. "LTE/LTE-A Network Security Data Collection and Analysis for Security Measurement: A Survey." In: *IEEE Access* 6 (2018), pages 4220-4242. ISSN: 2169-3536. DGI: 10.1109/access.2018.2792534. URL: https://ieeexplore.ieee.org/document/8255622.

[2] James HENRYDGSS and Terry BGULT. "Critical security review and study of DDoS attacks on LTE mobile network". In: *2014 IEEE Asia Pacific Conference on Wireless and Mobile.* IEEE, August 2014. DGI: 10.1109/apwimob.2014.6920286.

[3] Dmitry A. BARANGV, Aleksandr O. TEREKHIN, Dmitry S. BRAGIN and Artur A. MITSEL. "Simulation of DDoS Attacks on LTE and LoRaWAN Protocols in the NS-3 Network Simulator". In: *High-Performance Computing Systems and Technologies in Scientific Research, Automation of Control and Production.* Springer International Publishing, 2023, pages 291-301. ISBN : 9783031237447. DGI: 10.1007/978-3-031-23744-7_22. URL : https://link.springer.com/chapter/10.1007/978-3-031-23744-7_22.

[4] Jan FENG, Bing-Kai HGNG and Shin-Ming CHENG. "DDoS Attacks in Experimental LTE Networks". In: *Web, Artificial Intelligence and Network Applications.* Springer International Publishing, 2020, pages 545-553. ISBN: 9783030440381. DGI : 10.1007/978-3-030-44038-1_50.   URL   : https://link.springer.com/chapter/10.1007/978-3- 030-44038-1_50.

[5] *LTE Security Architecture.* Oct. 2012. DGI: 10.1002/9781118380642.ch6.

[6] 3RD GENERATIGN PARTNERSHIP PRGJECT; TECHNICAL SPECIFICATIGN GRGUP SERVICES AND SYSTEM ASPECTS. *Architecture Enhancement for Non-3GPP Accesses (Release 14).* 3GPP TS 23.402. Version V14.3.0. 3GPP, 2017. URL: https://www.etsi.org/deliver/etsi_ts/123400_123499/123402/14.03.00_60/ts_123 402v140300p. pdf.

[7] N. SINGH and M. S. SAINI. "A robust 4G/LTE network authentication for realization of flexible and robust security scheme". In: *2016 3rd International Conference on Computing for Sustainable Global Development (INDIACom).* IEEE. March 2016, pages 3211-3216. URL: https://ieeexplore.ieee.org/document/7724858.

[8] Jin CAG, Maode MA, Hui LI, Yueyu ZHANG and Zhenxing LUG. "A Survey on Security Aspects for LTE and LTE-A Networks." In: *IEEE Communications Surveys & Tutorials* 16.1 (2014), pages 283-302. ISSN: 1553-877X. DGI : 10.1109/surv.2013.041513. 00174.

[9] Siddharth Prakash RAG, Bhanu Teja KGTTE and Silke HOLTMANNS. "Privacy in LTE networks. In: *Proceedings of the 9th EAI International Conference on Mobile Multimedia Communications.* MOBIMEDIA. ACM, 2016. DGI: 10.4108/eai.18-6-

2016.2264393.

[10] S. HGLTMANNS, S. P. RAG and I. OLIVER. "User location tracking attacks for LTE networks using the interworking functionality". In: *Proc. IFIP Netw. Conf. Workshops.* IEEE, May 2016, pages 315-322. DGI: 10.1109/ifipnetworking.2016.7497239.

[11] R. P. JGVER, J. LACKEY and A. RAGHAVAN. "Enhancing the security of LTE networks against jamming attacks". In: *EURASIP J. Inf. Secur.* 2014.1 (Apr. 2014), pages 7-20. ISSN: 1687-417X. DGI: 10.1186/1687-417x-2014-7. URL: https://doi.org/10.1186/1687-417X-2014-7.

[12] M. LICHTMAN, R. P. JGVER, M. LABIB, R. RAG, V. MARGJEVIC and J. H. REED. "LTE/LTE-A jamming, spoofing, and sniffing: Threat assessment and mitigation". In: *IEEE Commun. Mag.* 54.4 (Apr. 2016), pages 54-61. ISSN : 0163-6804. DGI : 10.1109/mcom.2016.7452266.

[13] Farhan M. AZIZ, Jeff S. SHAMMA and Gordon L. STUBER. "Resilience of LTE networks against smart jamming attacks: Wideband model". In: *2015 IEEE 26th Annual International Symposium on Personal, Indoor, and Mobile Radio Communications (PIMRC).* IEEE, August 2015, pages 1344-1348. DGI: 10.1109/pimrc.2015.7343507.

[14] R. PIQUERAS JGVER. "Security Attacks Against the Availability of LTE Mobility Networks: Overview and Research Directions". In: *IEEE* (2015). Published online. URL: https://ieeexplore.ieee.org/document/6618585.

[15] Chan-Kyu HAN and Hyoung-Kee CHOI. "Security Analysis of Handover Key Management in 4G LTE/SAE Networks". In: *IEEE Transactions on Mobile Computing* 13.2 (Feb. 2014), pages 457-468. ISSN : 1536-1233. DGI : 10.1109/tmc.2012.242.

[16] Adrian DABRGWSKI, Nicola PIANTA, Thomas KLEPP, Martin MULAZZANI and Edgar WEIPPL, "IMSI-catch me if you can: IMSI-catcher-catchers". In: *Proceedings of the 30th Annual Computer Security Applications Conference.* ACSAC '14. ACM, Dec. 2014, pages 246-255. DGI: 10.1145/2664243.2664272.

[17] Patrick TRAYNOR, Michael LIN, Machigar ONGTANG, Vikhyath RAG, Trent JAEGER, Patrick MCDANIEL and Thomas LA PORTA. "On cellular botnets: measuring the impact of malicious devices on a cellular network core". In: *Proceedings of the 16th ACM conference on Computer and communications security.* CCS '09. ACM, Nov. 2009. DGI : 10.1145/1653662.1653690.

[18] Georgios KAMBQURAKIS, Constantinos KOLIAS, Stefanos GRITZALIS and Jong Hyuk PARK. "DoS attacks exploiting signaling in UMTS and IMS". In : *Computer Communications* 34.3 (March 2011), pages 226-235. ISSN : 0140-3664. DOI : 10.1016/j.comcom.2010.02.010.

[19] Seongmin PARK, Sekwon KIM, Kyungho SON and Hwankuk KIM. "Security Threats and

Countermeasure Frame Using a Session Control Mechanism on VoLTE". In: *2015 10th International Conference on Broadband and Wireless Computing, Communication and Applications (BWCCA)*. IEEE, 2015, pages 532-537. DOI: `10.1109/bwcca.2015.11`. URL: https://ieeexplore.ieee.org/document/7424882.

[20] Guan-Hua Tu, Chi-Yu Li, Chunyi Peng and Songwu Lu. "How voice call technology poses security threats in 4G LTE networks". In: *2015 IEEE Conference on Communications and Network Security (CNE)*. IEEE, Sept. 2015, pages 442-450. DOI: `10.1109/cns.2015.7346856`.

[21] J. Lee, K. Cho, C. Lee and S. Kim. "VoIP-aware network attack detection based on statistics and behavior of SIP traffic". In: *Peer-to-Peer Netw. Appl.* 8.5 (2015), pages 872880. URL: `https://link.springer.com/content/pdf/10.1007/s12083-014-0289- 8.pdf`.

[22] Guan-Hua Tu, Chi-Yu Li, Chunyi Peng, Yuanjie Li and Songwu Lu. "New Security Threats Caused by IMS-based SMS Service in 4G LTE Networks". In: *Proceedings of the 2016 ACM SIGSAC Conference on Computer and Communications Security*. CCS'16. ACM, Oct. 2016, pages 1118-1130. DOI: `10.1145/2976749.2978393`.

[23] S. Das, M. Pourzandi and M. Debbabi. "On SPIM detection in LTE networks". In: *2012 25th IEEE Canadian Conference on Electrical and Computer Engineering (CCECE)*. IEEE, Apr. 2012, pages 12-15. DOI: `10.1109/ccece.2012.6334959`.

[24] Chi-Yu Li, Guan-Hua Tu, Chunyi Peng, Zengwen Yuan, Yuanjie Li, Songwu Lu and Xinbing Wang. "Insecurity of Voice Solution VoLTE in LTE Mobile Networks". In: *Proceedings of the 22nd ACM SIGSAC Conference on Computer and Communications Security.* CCS'15. ACM, Oct. 2015, pages 316-327. DOI: `10.1145/2810103.2813618`.

[25] Chunyi Peng, Chi-Yu Li, Hongyi Wang, Guan-Hua Tu and Songwu Lu. "Real Threats to Your Data Bills: Security Loopholes and Defenses in Mobile Data Charging". In: *Proceedings of the 2014 ACM SIGSAC Conference on Computer and Communications Security.* CCS'14. ACM, Nov. 2014, pages 727-738. DOI: `10.1145/2660267.2660346`. URL: https://dl.acm.org/doi/10.1145/2660267.2660346.

[26] S. Ayyaz, M. A. Khan, J. Ahmad, C. Beard, B. Y. Choi and N. A. Saqib. "A novel security system for preventing DoS attacks on 4G LTE networks". In: *Proceedings of the International Conference on Wireless Networks (ICWN)*. The Steering Committee of The World Congress in Computer Science, Computer Engineering and Applied Computing (WorldComp). 2016, page 85. URL: `https://www.researchgate.net/publication/`

311367621_A_Novel_Security_System_for_Preventing_DoS_Attacks_on_4G_LTE_ Networks.

[27] Abdullah Ahmed BAHASHWAN, Mohammed ANBAR, Selvakumar MANICKAM, TaiefAlaa ALAMIEDY, Mohammad Adnan ALADAILEH and Iznan Husainy HASBULLAH. "A Systematic Literature Review on Machine Learning and Deep LearningApproaches for Detecting DDoS Attacks in Software-Defined Networking". In: *Sensors* 23.9 (2023), page 4441. DOI: 10.3390/S23094441.

[28] Himanshu SETIA, Amit CHHABRA, Sunil K. SINGH, Sudhakar KUMAR, Sarita SHARMA, Varsha ARYA, Brij B. GUPTA and Jinsong WU. "Securing the road ahead: machine learning-driven DDoS attack detection in VANET cloud environments". In: *Cyber Secur. Appl.* 2 (2024), page 100037. DOI: 10.1016/J.CSA.2024.100037.

[29] Dyari Mohammad SHARIF, Hakem BEITOLLAHI and Mahdi FAZELI. "Detection of ApplicationLayer DDoS Attacks Produced by Various Freely Accessible Toolkits Using Machine Lear- ning". In: *IEEEAccess* 11 (2023), pages 51810-51819. DOI : 10.1109/ACCESS.2023. 3280122.

[30] Josue Genaro ALMARAZ-RIVERA, Jesús Arturo Pérez DIAZ and Jose Antonio CANTORAL- CEBALLOS. "Transport and Application Layer DDoS Attacks Detection to IoT Devices by Using Machine Learning and Deep Learning Models". In: *Sensors* 22.9 (2022), page 3367. DOI: 10.3390/S22093367.

[31] Abdussalam Ahmed ALASHHAB, Mohd Soperi Mohd ZAHID, Mohamed A. AZIM, Muhammad Yunis DAHA, Babangida ISYAKU and Shimhaz ALI. "A Survey of Low Rate DDoS Detection Techniques Based on Machine Learning in Software-Defined Networks." In: *Symmetry* 14.8 (29 Jul. 2022). Edited by Yu-Chi CHEN, page 1563. ISSN: 2073-8994. DOI: 10.3390/sym14081563.

[32] Khatereh AHMADI and Reza JAVIDAN. "DDoS Attack Detection in a Real Urban IoT Environment Using Federated Deep Learning". In: Venice, Italy. Venice, Italy: IEEE, 2023, pages 117-122. ISBN : 979-8-3503-1171-6. DOI : 10.1109/CSR57506.2023.10224916.

[33] Monika ROOPAK, Gui Yun TIAN and Jonathon CHAMBERS. "Deep Learning Models for Cyber Security in IoT Networks". In: Las Vegas, NV, USA. Las Vegas, NV, USA: IEEE, 2019, pages 0452-0457. ISBN: 978-1-7281-0555-0. DOI: 10.1109/CCWC.2019.8666588.

[34] B. B. GUPTA, Akshat GAURAV and Dragan PERAKOVIC. "A Big Data and Deep Learning based Approach for DDoS Detection in Cloud Computing Environment". In: Kyoto, Japan. Kyoto, Japan : IEEE, 2021, pages 287-290. ISBN : 978-1-6654-3677-9. DOI : 10.1109/GCCE53005.2021.9622091.

[35]   *CICIDS2017   Intrusion   Detection   Evaluation   Dataset.* https://www.kaggle.com/datasets/ cicdataset/cicids2017/. Accessed on: <date>.

[36]   Faisal HUSSAIN, Syed Ghazanfar ABBAS, Muhammad HUSNAIN, Ubaid U. FAYYAZ, Farrukh SHAHZAD and Ghalib A. SHAH. "IoT DoS and DDoS Attack Detection using ResNet". In: (Dec. 2020), pages 1-6. DOI: 10.21203/rs.3.rs-120303/v1.

[37]   R. J. ALZAHRANI and A. ALZAHRANI. "Security analysis of DDoS attacks using machine learning algorithms in network traffic". In: *Electronics* 10 (2021), page 2919. DOI: 10.3390/electronics10242919.

[38]   T. DHAMOR, S. BHAT and S. THENMALAR. "Dynamic approaches for detection of DDoS threats using machine learning". In: *Ann. Rom. Soc. Cell Biol.* 2021 (2021), pages 1366313673.

[39]   R. AMRISH, K. BAVAPRIYAN, V. GOPINAATH, A. JAWAHAR and C.V. KUMAR. "DDoS detection using machine learning techniques". In: *J. IOT Soc. Mobile, Anal. Cloud* 4 (2022), pages 24-32. DOI: 10.1007/s13174-021-00347-6.

[40]   K. KUMARI and M. MRUNALINI. "Detecting Denial of Service attacks using machine learning algorithms". In: *J. Big Data* 9 (2022), page 56. DOI: 10.1186/s40537-022-00530-8.

[41]   C. NALAYINI and J. KATIRAVAN. "Detection of DDoS Attack Using Machine Learning Algorithms". In: *SSRN* 9 (2022), page 4173187.

[42]   R. QAMAR, B. ZARDARI, A. ARAIN, F. KHOSO and A. JOKHIO. "Detecting Distributed Denial of Service attacks using Recurrent Neural Network". In: *Psychology* 2022 (2022), page 1.

[43]   I. ULLAH and Q.H. MAHMOUD. "Design and development of RNN anomaly detection model for IoT networks". In: *IEEE Access* 10 (2022), pages 62722-62750. DOI: 10.1109/ACCESS.2022.3220238.

[44]   S. HARIPRASAD, T. DEEPA and N. BHARATHiRAjA. "Detection of DDoS Attack in IoT Networks Using Sample Selected RNN-ELM". In: *Intell. Autom. Soft Comput.* 34 (2022), page 17. DOI: 10.5879/ijst.2022.22.17.

[45]   Siva Sarat KONA. "Detection of DDoS attacks using RNN-LSTM and Hybrid model ensemble". PhD thesis. Dublin, National College of Ireland, 2020. URL: https://norma.ncirl.ie/4180/1/sivasaratkona.pdf.

[46]   Asha Varma SONGA and Ganesh Redy KARRI. "Ensemble-RNN: A Robust Framework for DDoS Detection in Cloud Environment". In : *Majlesi Journal of Electrical Engineering* 17.4

(2023), pages 31-44. URL: `https:// journals . iau . ir / article _ 705412 _ 14633e4d9bb5ab0eed6c014b510cc43d.pdf`.

[47] K. SAURABH, S. SOOD, P.A. KUMAR, U. SINGH, R. VYAS, O. VYAS and R. KHONDOKER. "Lbdmids: LSTM based deep learning model for intrusion detection systems for IOT networks". In: *Proceedings of the 2022 IEEE World AI IoT Congress (AIIoT)*. 2022, pages 753-759.

[48] R. QAMAR. "Gradient Techniques to Predict Distributed Denial-Of-Service Attack". In: *Iraqi J. Comput. Sci. Math.* 3 (2022), pages 55-71. DOI: `10.25677/ijcsm-63`.

[49] R. QAMAR, A. A. ARAIN, K. KANWAR, F. H. KHOSO and F. JOKHIO. "Distributed Denial Of Service Attack Detection Based On Neural Network: A Comparative Study". In: *Int. J. Sci. Technol. Res.* 2 (2022), page 15.

[50] M. A. RAHMAN. "Detection of distributed denial of service attacks based on machine learning algorithms". In: *Int. J. Smart Home* 14 (2020), pages 15-24. DOi: `10.5579/ ijsh.2020.v14n2p15`.

[51] M. RUSYAIDI, S. JAF and Z. IBRAHIM. "Detecting distributed denial of service in network traffic with deep learning". In: *Int. J. Adv. Comput. Sci. Appl.* 13 (2022), pages 34-41. DOI `:10.14569/ijacsa.2022.013.0405`.

[52] J. COSTA, N. DESSAI, S. GAONKAR, S. ASWALE and P. SHETGAONKAR. "IoT-botnet detection using long short-term memory recurrent neural network". In: *Int. J. Eng. Res* 9 (2020), page 18. DOi: `10.21275/9954`.

[53] F. M. ASWAD, A. M. S. AHMED, N. A. M. ALHAMMADI, B. A. KHALAF and S. A. MOSTAFA. "Deep learning in distributed denial-of-service attacks detection method for Internet of Things networks". In: *J. Intell. Syst.* 32 (2023), page 20220155. DOI : `10.1007/s10844-022-0733-6`.

[54] Iman SHARAFALDIN, Saqib HAKAK, Arash HabibiLASHKARi and AГiGHGRBAN. *CIC-DDoS2019 Dataset.* https://www . kaggle . com/datasets/dhoogla/cicddos2019. Accessed on [date]. 2019.

[55] Iman SHARAFALDIN, Arash HabibiLASHKARi, Saqib HAKAK and AliA. GHGRBANI. "Developing Realistic Distributed Denial of Service (DDoS) Attack Dataset and Taxonomy". In: *2019 International Carnahan Conference on Security Technology (ICCST)*. IEEE, 2019, pages 1-8. DGI: 10.1109/ccst.2019.8888419.

[56] *Normalization.* URL: https : / / www . digitalocean . com/ community/ tutorials/ normalize-data-in-python (visited 04/02/2023).

[57] UNKNOWN. *Categorical Data.* 2020. URL: https://www.kdnuggets.com/2021/05/ deal-with-categorical-data-machine-learning.html (visited 09/09/2020).

[58]   *Testing Split Method in Machine Learning.* Accessed on 12 December 2022. URL : https: //www.researchgate.net/post/70_training_and_30_testing_spit_method_in_ machine_learning.

[59]   TECHTARGET. *Data Splitting,* URL: https://www.techtarget.com/searchenterpriseai/ definition/datasplitting (visited 04/02/2024),

[60]   Ahamed Ali SAMSU ALIAR and Moorthy AGGRAMGGRTHY, "An Automated Detection of DDoS Attack in Cloud Using Optimized Weighted Fused Features and Hybrid DBN- GRU Architecture", In: *Cybernetics and Systems* (2022), pages 1-42, DGI: 10.1080/ 01969722.2022.2157603,

[61]   Rekha GANGULA, V Murali MGHAN and Ranjeeth KUMAR, "A comprehence study of DDoS attack detecting algorithm using GRU-BWFA classifier", In : *Measurement : Sensors* 24 (2022), page 100570, DGI : 10.1016/j.measen.2022.100570,

[62]   Saif ur REHMAN, Mubashir KHALIQ, Syed Ibrahim IMTIAZ, Aamir RASGGL, Muhammad SHAFIQ, Abdul Rehman JAVED, Zunera JALIL and Ali Kashif BASHIR, "DIDDOS: An approach for detection and identification of Distributed Denial of Service (DDoS) cyberattacks using Gated Recurrent Units (GRU)", In: *Future Generation Computer Systems* 118 (2021), pages 453-466, DGI: 10.1016/j.future.2021.01.022,

[63]   M, H, H, KHAIRI, S, H, S, ARIFFIN, N, M, ABDUL LATIFF, A, S, ABDULLAH and M, K, HASSAN, "A Review of Anomaly Detection Techniques and Distributed Denial of Service (DDoS) on Software Defined Network (SDN)", In: *Engineering, Technology & Applied Science Research* 8,2 (Apr, 2018), pages 2724-2730, ISSN: 2241-4487, DGI: 10.48084/etasr . 1840, URL: https: //etasr . com/index . php/ETASR/article/ view/1840/pdf,

[64] Brij B GUPTA, Kwok Tai CHUI, Akshat GAURAV and Varsha ARYA. "GRU-Based DDoS Detection for Enhanced Security in Consumer Electronics". In: *2023 IEEE 13th International Conference on Consumer Electronics-Berlin (ICCE-Berlin).* IEEE. 2023, pages 1-4. DOI: 10.1109/icce-berlin58801.2023.10375584.

Buy your books fast and straightforward online - at one of world's fastest growing online book stores! Environmentally sound due to Print-on-Demand technologies.

Buy your books online at
www.morebooks.shop

Kaufen Sie Ihre Bücher schnell und unkompliziert online – auf einer der am schnellsten wachsenden Buchhandelsplattformen weltweit! Dank Print-On-Demand umwelt- und ressourcenschonend produziert.

Bücher schneller online kaufen
www.morebooks.shop

Printed by Books on Demand GmbH, Norderstedt / Germany